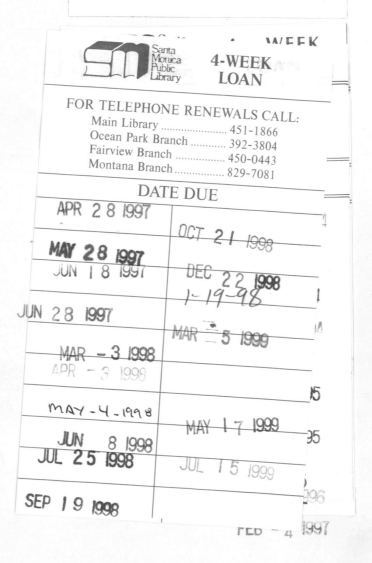

The Inner Harmony of
the **JAPANESE HOUSE**

The Inner Harmony of the JAPANESE HOUSE

Atsushi Ueda

with an introduction by Gunter Nitschke

KODANSHA INTERNATIONAL
Tokyo and New York

NOTE: Japanese names for historical figures (pre–1868) are given in the traditional Japanese manner—that is, surname preceding given name—since they are still discussed in current literature in that way. All other names appear in the western order. A chart of Japanese historical periods is given at the end of this volume.

Translated from the original Japanese edition of *Nihonjin to sumai* published by Iwanami Shoten. The initial translation was done by Stephen Suloway.

Distributed in the United States by Kodansha International/USA Ltd., 114 Fifth Avenue, New York, New York. Published by Kodansha International Ltd., 17–14 Otowa 1-chome, Bunkyo-ku, Tokyo 112 and Kodansha International/USA Ltd., 114 Fifth Avenue, New York, New York 10011.

Library of Congress Cataloguing-in-Publication Data
Ueda, Atsushi 1930–
    [Nihonjin to sumai, English]
    The inner harmony of the Japanese house/by Atsushi Ueda: with an introduction by Gunter Nitschke.–1st ed.
        Translation of: Nihonjin to sumai/Ueda Atsushi
    1. Architecture, Domestic–Japan. 2. Room layout (Dwellings)–Japan. 3. Shoji screens–Japan. I. Nitschke, Gunter. II Title.
    NA7451.U3313   1990   728'.0952–dc20   90-4310 CIP

First edition, 1990
ISBN 0-87011-934-6
ISBN 4-7700-1434-1 (Japan)

Contents

Preface

It is now fifteen years since the first Japanese edition of this book came out. At that time I set out to chart a course for the Japanese residence of the future, including historical and climatic perspectives as well as utilitarian considerations. I chose a format of two dozen short essays with the general reader in mind, but I also intended to address architectural specialists by drawing on my many years of research on the traditional townhouses of Japanese tradespeople. Overall, I wanted to present a fresh look at the modern Japanese home within a historical perspective.

I'm now gratified that in the past decade and a half many of the recommendations I espoused in the book have actually been implemented. In contrast to the westernization trend that was in full-swing at the time, the Japanese home has now made a comeback on its own merits—not just from nostalgia.

It is my hope that this translation will appeal to a large audience of foreign readers since this book presents a discussion of Japanese culture as seen from the perspective of its dwellings. I appreciate the efforts of editor Shigeyoshi Suzuki in supplementing the book with a significant number of appropriate illustrations to help the foreign reader understand more clearly the elements of Japanese design. I sincerely wish that this book will be appreciated as widely abroad as it has been in Japan.

Atsushi Ueda
Kyoto

Introduction

Gunter Nitschke

Over the past century and a half much has been written in the West about Japanese architecture, especially about the Japanese home. Nearly all of these observations were made by westerners who were critical of the architecture as often as they were laudatory. "The first sight of a Japanese home is disappointing; it is unsubstantial in appearance and there is a meagerness of color," wrote Edward Sylvester Morse in his *Japanese Homes and Their Surroundings*. This book, published in 1886, became the first western classic on the subject. It is still in print today. The author surveyed the Japanese dwelling and the daily lives of its occupants before the large-scale adaptation of western architectural values and forms.

In 1937, Bruno Taut in *Houses and People of Japan* wrote, "Simplicity almost to the point of poverty is the essential basis of Japanese aesthetics. Such being the case, it is quite logical that the Japanese house should not be packed with furniture." It is this theme of "simplicity," "emptiness," and "openness to nature" that runs through his discussions of not only traditional Japanese farmhouses—but even of shrines, teahouses and palaces. His work has played a catalytic role in establishing the Ise Grand Shrine and the Katsura Detached Palace as important components of world architecture. Taut elevated the discourse on the Japanese house from a folkloric level to that of an aesthetic program of the modern movement.

The next milestone publication on the Japanese house was Heinrich Engel's *The Japanese House—A Tradition for Contemporary Architecture*, in 1964. It became a classic because of its detailed presentation of the wooden joinery techniques and its discussion of the modular system of the fully developed Japanese dwelling. In particular, the two chapters on "Measure and Construction of the Japanese House" are renowned for their exact technical drawings and scholarship. These two chapters were reprinted separately from the main work in 1985.

In 1980 Chris Fawcett presented an innovative and intriguing perspective of the Japanese house in *The New Japanese House—Ritual and Antiritual—Pattern of Development* by merging the concepts of the traditional and the modern house. With this unique turn of perspective, he shed new light on the formal and theoretical complexities of the traditional as well as the post-Metabolical house, analyzing them in terms of their ''ritual affirming'' and ''ritual disaffirming'' qualities.

Now entering the fray is the Japanese author and scholar of traditional Japanese urban architecture, Atsushi Ueda. With a sense of humor as well as a sense of the pragmatic necessities of everyday life, Ueda dismantles the last remnants of the mystique of the Japanese house. For Ueda, it has often sacrificed human comfort, structural development and spatial variety to a doubtful restrictive canon of aesthetics. The Japanese dwelling in Ueda's opinion is not an object of aesthetic or structural admiration, nor is it an expression of the mindscape of its designers. Although he grew up in the homes he criticizes, he displays no prejudice in favor of or against the traditional or the modern house. He exhibits no nostalgia for the past.

''The contemporary Japanese house, caught between tradition and modernism,'' he writes, ''is nervously confessing its own insecurity.'' He acknowledges that the traditional house is full of cracks and is badly lit. Moreover, it never developed a livable and fully usable second floor throughout its entire history. On the other hand, he points out that it is unique in its various inventions, especially those involving the veranda and the eaves. The tatami flooring presents an extraordinary sensitivity to him. And he cannot help but to notice the beautifully shaped roofscapes unfolding in a certain splendor.

''The traditional Japanese house is dead,'' Ueda contends, echoing Nietzsche's ''God is dead.'' In a sense, Ueda himself has killed the myth. The strength of Ueda's book lies in the fact that it addresses reality. *The Inner Harmony of the Japanese House* originally appeared as a paperback in 1974 with the title *Nihonjin to sumai*. Having sold over 300,000 copies, the book apparently has attracted many non-architects among its readers. Although the book is now a bit dated in some respects, this translation is still on the whole a refreshing insight into both the frailties and strengths of the Japanese house. Some of Ueda's prophesies have come true, and some of his fears realized; others have dissipated. Today, Ueda actually is not as pessimistic as he was in 1974. Like a phoenix, the traditional Japanese house, or at least elements of the traditional house, seems to be rising from the ashes. The sloped roof, the decorative alcove and other elements of the traditional Japanese house are harmoniously being melded with modern design.

One can only wish that not "the house" but "housing," traditional or modern, will become the new focus of attention. Even though "housing" has been on center stage throughout the Modern movement in Europe, it has not yet even begun to emerge as a subject of either design or critical theoretical discourse in Japan. Perhaps Ueda's next book will address this issue.

Gunter Nitschke
Kyoto

Pillars

T he history of European architecture is the history of the struggle with the window,'' commented Le Corbusier (1887–1965), a leading architect of our century. If I paraphrased his words to apply to Japan, I would have to say, ''The history of Japanese architecture is the history of the struggle with the pillar.'' The European architect's confrontation with windows stemmed from the European reliance on stone and brick construction. It is easy to build high walls, but it is hard to make openings for windows because of the sheer weight of the stone and brick, which bears down on the lintels. The Japanese, on the other hand, had to confront a problem which at first glance seemed trivial, but in fact proved difficult. They found significant obstacles trying to erect perpendicular building elements, especially as the primary material used was almost always wood.

Since Japan was a country of forests, it was natural that wood was the basic building material. The reliance on wood necessitated sound pillars, especially since Japan is earthquake-prone and has high humidity most of the year.

To begin with, there is a symbolic dimension to the pillar in Japanese architecture. For example, *tenchi kongen tsukuri* (literally translated as the ''palace construction of heaven and earth'') was an early style that incorporated the idea of the symbolic pillar. Knowledge of this design has been passed down among carpenters since ancient times. It was probably a type of pit dwelling derived from the ancient housing that was constructed over a hole in the ground. In the early house design two poles were erected at an appropriate distance from each other, then a ridgepole was placed across them and logs were leaned up against the ridgepole and interlocked at the top. This is the steep-rafter style known as *gassho-zukuri* (literally, ''praying hands'' style), which looks more or

Izumo Shrine: an ancient example of a raised structure.

less like a gabled roof placed directly on the ground. Needless to say, the essential element of the structure was the pillar; if a pillar broke or fell, then the whole structure (heaven and earth) came crashing down instantly. The pillar was the linchpin of the house.

There is some question as to whether such dwellings actually existed, but if such a structure were lifted up and placed on a square room with a floor raised off the ground, it would look a lot like the oldest Shinto shrine building in Japan, the Izumo Shrine in Shimane Prefecture. In the center of this inner shrine building there is a pillar called the *shin no mihashira* (''esteemed pillar of the heart''). At the centers of the front and back gable walls there are also pillars, and these three pillars form a line to support the ridgepole. These pillars, called *uzubashira*, resemble the freestanding ridge-supporting pillars which are found at the similarly ancient Ise Shrine in Mie Prefecture.

Gegu, one of the Ise Shrine buildings, utilizes ridge supporting pillars (*uzubashira*).

Today, when we think of building with pillars, we usually think of a boxlike construction on the pattern of a bird cage. In the remains of ancient pit dwellings from the prehistoric Jomon (10,000 B.C.–300 B.C.) and Yayoi (300 B.C.–A.D. 300) periods there is evidence of four pillars, resembling a table, with the roof rafters leaned up against its four sides. More generally, in the later development of Japanese architecture, the form which became more and more predominant was a delicate box-shaped construction. But still, we know that there was also that pattern of the thick ridgepole under a heavy roof, directly supported by a row of pillars. This system, incidentally, was surprisingly stable during earthquakes because the pillars were sunk deeply into the ground.

Aside from earthquakes, the residents of pit dwellings had to put up with dampness and the damage that dampness could cause. In Japan, where the underground water table is high, the base of a sunken post

Horyuji: a five-story pagoda and the oldest wooden structure in the world.
Early 7th century.

rots easily. This made it likely that if an earthquake occurred, the base would crumble or break away from the pillar. To prevent this the Japanese learned from the Chinese, around the 8th century, to place a foundation stone in the ground and mount the pillar on top of it. As this technique spread, damage from rotting was greatly reduced.

The building not only rested on a single row of pillars down the center, but the pillars were also not firmly embedded in the earth. Although this would appear to be less stable than the embedded-pillar design, it actually provided ample stability in an earthquake, on the same principle that allows a person to temporarily balance an upright baseball bat in the palm of his hand by regularly moving his hand back and forth to compensate for the swaying of the bat. This is one of the wonders of Japanese architecture. This principle was further refined in the past few hundred years, in the construction of multistory structures such as a five-story pagoda or Himeji Castle in Hyogo Prefecture. In either case, most of the building's weight was borne by four pillars resting on foundation stones which were at ground level. When an earthquake occurred, the violent shock was softened and the building merely rocked slowly back and forth.

This theory has been largely implemented in residential structures. The typical farmhouse or townhouse has either a main pillar (a *daikokubashira*) at the center of the building or a row of three pillars concentrated on that central point, supporting most of the weight of the roof. If an earthquake occurs, the same sort of balancing trick is automatically performed, preventing the building from collapsing. The technique resembles the modern style of architecture in which a thick wall or thick pillars are constructed at the core of the structure of the building so that the outer walls can be made entirely of suspended glass or other nonstructural material. When this is done, most of the pillars are freed from bearing the load of the building, with the exception of the central pillar and a few other structural pillars. It then becomes possible to designate the non–load-bearing pillars as "furnishing pillars" for such functions as interior decoration, partitions, window frames and door frames.

The beautiful woodwork which characterizes Japanese interiors is based on measurements which do not deviate by even a millimeter. Such fine workmanship could not have been developed without the existence of the furnishing pillars, which had been freed from bearing the load of the building.

But the architecture of modern wooden structures is often fundamentally different from that of the traditional style. In a modern wooden

The main pillar of a Japanese house (*daikokubashira*), resting on a stone foundation.

A *daikokubashira* (arrow) supporting a complex series of rafters and struts.

A decorative alcove pillar (*takobashira*) and other "furnishing pillars."

building, a wooden ground sill is placed on top of a concrete foundation, and on top of that a sort of ''box'' of posts, beams, girders and other elements is erected. These ''boxes'' are strengthened with angle braces. Since the connections are mostly made by using nails or bolts, traditional Japanese joinery techniques of cutting notches into lumber are now disappearing. The newer technique is structurally quite sound. The structure is supported by the rigidity of each face of the ''box,'' and of the beams and braces which are placed horizontally or diagonally. Thus the role of the pillar in the building is reduced to that of a simple perpendicular element. Although this is a great loss of status for the Japanese pillar, it is not necessarily a loss to grieve over, since the structural revision has given the building more strength to withstand earthquakes.

The precision required in the fashioning of a structural element and that of a furnishing element is quite different. In the case of a structural element, a joint between, say, a pillar and a beam may come loose to some extent, but as long as it does not come apart it is still sound. During an earthquake it may be even more sound because the play allows it to work as a shock absorber. A nail or bolt eats into the body of the wood, and this normally causes loosening to some extent. When the pillar is considered as a furnishing element, a gap—even a gap of, say, three millimeters (0.012 inch)—is a problem. If a door or window cannot be completely closed, rain or wind may enter, causing the quality of day-to-day life to deteriorate. In fact, wooden houses in Japan today have mostly degenerated to this sort of tacky construction. The pillar receives not only the dual burdens of structure and furnishing, but it is also pierced by nails and bolts. In homes that have been standing for decades, the doors and sliding panels work quite smoothly, but in recently built wooden homes, cracks appear here and there after two or three years and the doors and windows no longer close correctly. It makes one wonder what on earth the designers were thinking about.

The Japanese word for pillar, *hashira*, is not limited to architecture. In Japanese, it is often used as a pronoun to refer to the core of things. The head of a household is also called the *daikokubashira* (central pillar) and the gist of a policy is called the *hashira* (a pillar). But it goes further than that. From ancient times, the word to count gods has been *hashira*. In fact, the use of the word *hashira* to indicate the core or mainstay of something is deeply related to the gods. It is said that the ancient Japanese religion which later became the Shinto religion was founded on a belief in the divinity of trees. This is because the tree was thought of as a *yorishiro*, or a means by which the gods descended to earth. Old trees which had been struck by lightning often became objects of worship, this being viewed as concrete proof that there were places where the gods descended. Later, the *yorishiro* became the original shape of the Shinto shrine. The *shin no mihashira* (esteemed pillar of the heart) under the center of the floor of the main temple of the Ise Shrine in Mie Prefecture is merely a round pillar about one and a half meters (five feet) high that has no significance whatsoever to the structure. It is significant because it is regarded as a *yorishiro* in which the gods reside.

The pillar in Japanese architecture is probably the last vestige of ancient tree worship. It may even be possible that the existence of Japanese architecture in which pillars are lined up in a single row in the center of the building is related to the significance of this *yorishiro*. And conversely, this may be what has given the pillar its importance in Japanese architecture. When the pillar was made into an object of worship, people recognized its potential significance in other ways as well. Even now, in old households, the god of the house is thought to reside in a pillar. In a tradesman's home, the children may not be allowed to so much as lean against the central pillar. The New Year custom of attaching pine fronds and a straw rope to the central pillar, and placing offerings of rice wine and *mochi* (pounded rice) before it, still survives.

Thus we see that the pillar has been useful to the Japanese in various ways. But today the central pillar stands virtually removed from modern construction. Furthermore, there has recently been a switch from *shinkabe* construction, in which the wall is placed between exposed pillars, to *okabe* construction, in which the pillars are enclosed in mortar inside the wall in order to prevent fires. Thus the pillar is gradually receding from view. Having long functioned as the key structural element, and having for centuries assumed the additional role of an influential furnishing element, the pillar has rather suddenly fallen into neglect. What we are witnessing is the elimination of the pillar from Japanese architecture.

If one accepts the pillar in modern construction as a structural member of the entire building, then he should think about it as having the function of a window frame or a door frame. Since window frames and door frames have been elaborately installed using time-honored carpentry traditions, it doesn't matter if the pillars are buried away in the walls, or if, like the *tokobashira* (the pillar on one side of the *tokonoma* alcove; see Chapter 9), they are regarded as purely decorative. In European and American homes the window frames and door frames are installed first; then the doors and windows, with their sashes already enclosed, are brought in on trucks and simply slapped into place in the brick walls. Therefore, rarely are gaps left between the frames and the window sashes or doors. Since the structure of the modern Japanese wooden home has changed from the former "*hashira* construction" (post-and-beam) and is now reinforced with joints and braces, it has become a type of "wall construction" in the same manner as in European and American brick architecture. As a result, the flexibility of Japanese house design has increased since a door or window need not necessarily be placed next to a pillar; it can be freely placed within the room where it can be most conveniently used.

The offhanded downgrading of the pillar to a petty role is, in my opinion, a bigger source of potential problems than its outright elimination.

Roofs

The history of the modernization of Japanese architecture can be called the history of the elimination of the roof. Here we are referring to the sloped roof and not the flat top of a building that is often referred to as the "flat roof."

The modern buildings we see now in Japan made of reinforced concrete, irrespective of whether they are multistory office buildings, apartment buildings or individual houses, are nearly all without proper roofs.

By that definition, most office buildings and apartment blocks in Japan lack proper roofs, as do modern houses, especially those of reinforced concrete construction. Looking back at the first wave of modern buildings, especially the western-style brick buildings from around the turn of the century, we do find sloped roofs. Perhaps that is why Meiji-era (1868–1912) buildings have such an old-fashioned air about them.

Until recently, Japanese architecture displayed roof designs which were graceful and elegant. The language of the common people includes words for all sorts of gabled roofs, hipped roofs and hipped gable roofs, as well as for various types of roof ornamentation such as *onigawara* (ridge-end sculptures of devils or spirits), *chigi* (crisscross projecting decorations), *katsuogi* (horizontal ridgetop molding) and *udatsu* (projecting walls to separate the roofs of two adjoining buildings). Anyone who has visited the Japanese countryside understands how charming and substantial a thatch-roofed farmhouse looks in the distance, with the eaves hanging down so far that it seems as if the roof is all there is to the structure. Japanese architecture is roofs, whereas western architecture is walls. It is sad indeed that the siren call of "modernization" is leaving fewer and fewer Japanese-style roofed structures.

In the Japanese context, modernization has more or less meant

Chigi and *katsuogi* roof embellishments of Izumo Shrine.

Ridge ornamentation of a thatched roof.

Ridge-end sculptures depicting a demon's face (*onigawara*).

A traditional thatched-roof farmhouse.

Traditional sloped roofs of a farming community.

westernization, or at least falling under western influence. But in Europe, the majority of new apartment buildings have sloped roofs. The "new towns" of Scandinavia and England are prime examples. Undoubtedly the sloped roofs are there largely for practical reasons. The shape allows for an attic space which can perform as a thermal buffer zone both summer and winter to serve as a storage space and, most important of all, provide positive drainage to keep out rain. In addition sloped roofs help prevent significant amounts of snow from accumulating, easing the threat of structural collapse. Naturally, sloped roofs are decidedly better than flat ones for water drainage. If a sloped roof is damaged, it is often possible to repair just the defective section. That is not the case for a typical flat roof of lightweight concrete over asphalt. Once water has leaked through this type of roof, the whole thing often has to be peeled up, which is a major operation.

When Japan established its public housing corporations after the war, those corporations gained a reputation for constructing buildings with leaky roofs. Decades later, the problem still exists in some of their buildings, and even in other modern structures. A friend of mine worked for a construction research institute with offices in a three-story ferroconcrete building. It leaked whenever it rained, the whole year round. The building was full of architects, and they tried everything short of replacing the top of the building, but to no avail. It seems that the building had deteriorated to the stage where nothing could be done about it. Although the shortness of the life of this building may be an exception, it is still important to consider the problems of the durability of ferroconcrete structures if even a few such buildings do not last thirty years. One might assume that because asphalt waterproofing works in swimming pools, it should surely work on rooftops. But the rooftop is the part of the building most susceptible to weathering, and various types of long-term wear-and-tear have to be factored into the calculations.

Flat roofs are common in arid zones of the world, such as countries around the Mediterranean or in non-tropical Africa. In rainy England or in snowy Scandinavia, most buildings have sloped roofs. Such roofs used to be common in Japan, a country which lies mostly in the monsoon belt and where substantial rainfall occurs in other seasons as well. It seems clear that coping with rain was a major consideration in the construction of Japanese dwellings from time immemorial. Since that is the case, why is it that along with "modernization" buildings have lost their roofs? Rain is not the only problem, either. Those people living on top floors under flat rooftops are forced to endure radiant heat in the hot, humid summers, a problem that even air conditioning cannot always adequately correct.

One reason architects have abandoned the sloped roof is that it has no place in the "modern" aesthetic. But what exactly, then, is meant by "modern"?

Europeans had long dreamed of being able to make artificial stone, and this was more or less accomplished in France in the mid-19th century with the marriage of iron rods and concrete. The result was a major revolution in construction techniques. Until then, people all over the world had laboriously utilized whatever building materials they had— stone, brick, wood, mud and so on. With the advent of reinforced concrete, it suddenly became much easier to erect lighter-weight, strong buildings. Moreover, since concrete can be cast and molded into virtually any shape, it allows extremely economical construction, most often in the simple geometry of the matchbox-type design.

Since sand, cement, iron or steel are readily obtainable in most nations, this type of building followed not only economic but also universal principles. It became known as the International Style. Existing buildings and their embellishments came to be perceived as old-fashioned; people began to think of the geometric pattern which was faithful mainly to economics as the Modern Style.

The "matchbox" design certainly caught on for multistory buildings, but it did not gain popularity as a design for detached residences. Homeowners preferred the traditional sloped roofs. The flat-roof matchbox design did appear in the experiments of the minimal house and the standardized house, which were conceived amid the severe housing problems in Germany after World War I. These styles underwent remarkable development after World War II, as they were adapted to millions of middle- and upper-class "modern living" homes erected in the American Midwest and West. These houses, which became part of the lifestyle of a new era, the American Style, were introduced to the world through photographic magazines. Needless to say, the Japanese, who had little that was new, quickly embraced the style.

But was this style, which took shape in the moderately dry zones of Central Europe and North America, a natural choice as something "modern" or "beautiful" in warmer and wetter climes as well? To this day, a sloped roof is considered an indispensable element of a house in England, a country which has a climate rather similar to that of Japan. In Northern Europe, there are many beautiful apartment buildings with sloping roofs. Even in America, the sloped roof has made something of a comeback not only for detached residences but also for apartment buildings. All in all, it seems that the "matchbox style" residences exist only in certain parts of the world and are, as yet, no more than a superficial phenomenon.

Another reason why the sloped roof is disappearing from Japanese architecture is the height limits imposed by building codes. Since the height of a building is measured from the peak of a sloped roof, some people lop off the roof in order to squeeze in a little more space. This is not unreasonable, since for years now land values have been soaring at an eye-popping rate. But this tendency to flatten roofs should be carefully reexamined in the future. If the height restrictions are the result of structural limitations in an earthquake zone, it should be realized that sloped roofs do not in themselves present problems of stability. If the goal of the regulation is to ensure sunlight exposure to neighboring lots, then the angle and direction of a sloped roof can be designed in accordance with the incidence of the sun so as to present only minimal interference. One possibility which deserves consideration is to exclude the roof portion of the building in measurements to determined the legal height. If the attic is used for storage or other functions and restrictions

Bird's-eye view of traditional tiled roofs in Kyoto.

are placed on it for use as living quarters, the result would not be lower-quality construction. Rather it would be possible to increase the usable space while also providing thermal insulation for the rooms beneath the roof and more effectively preventing water leakage.

Of course, when a sloping roof is erected, the view from the building directly behind is blocked to some extent. Yet the tops of most flat-roofed buildings are rather unattractive if not downright ugly. On the other hand, a gentle townscape of successive sloped tile roofs would add charm to the urban vista.

From ancient times tile roofs were mounted on temples and castles, but it was only during the last two or three centuries that the homes of common people had tile roofs. Tile roofs had been directly prohibited in order to preserve the class stratification system. Their cost indirectly prohibited their use by common people at that time. In addition, during the frequent wars of the 15th and 16th centuries, the wooden houses of the castle towns were often razed to the ground, not only by enemies but sometimes even by the lord of the castle. Thus the common man's house was enforcedly a poor affair, roofed either with wood shingles or thatch. The impoverished residents were tormented by summer heat, winter cold, leaking rain and the fear of fire or earthquake. It was not

Nishi Hongan-ji Hiunkaku (17th century): a *shoin*-style house with
a harmonious mixture of roof types.

Aerial view of modern Shinjuku Ward, Tokyo, with its hodge-podge architecture.

until the 18th century that, as a result of a pervading peace, improvement in the economic circumstances of the masses and the progress of urbanization, the prohibition was lifted and tile roofs became common. With the charming tile roofs, which did not leak and which reduced the fear of fire, even the shanty towns took on solid, respectable, if not quaint, appearances.

Whether it is based on conscious conceptions of history or design, the Japanese even today tend to have a deep longing for the good, old, sloped roof. For example, although neither government-developed apartment buildings nor most private-sector apartment blocks typically have sloped roofs, architects have often incorporated techniques that present an illusion of a proper roof—either the railings or other elements on the rooftop are slanted to look like a sloped roof from below, or else a gable has been attached to the penthouse. A distin-

Examples of very recent apartment buildings with sloped roofs.

guishing characteristic of publicly constructed apartment complexes is that they do not even have such a "simulated roof." Townscapes that look like rows of matchboxes are indeed dreary, and it is natural that they are frequently denigrated as "tombstone forests" or "prison blocks." It seems that the architects and bureaucrats have conspired to do away with the traditional roofs of this country's houses, but that just makes people want them all the more.

It is time for a reassessment. We are abandoning the sloping roof that was embedded in our history and required by our climate, and pursuing the flat roof in the name of something called "modernism." The building codes merely ratify trends which have originated on other continents. Surely Japan is capable of rational modernization that matches this country's climate, if we would only set our sights on it. The roof would be an excellent place to start.

Walls

Recently a British architectural scholar visiting Japan made a thorough investigation of Japanese housing and concluded, "In short, the homes are all austere." Underlying this statement is a feeling that the Japanese home does little to fulfill the function of a shelter with respect to summer heat and winter cold. Indeed since ancient times that has been a major deficiency of the Japanese home. But heat and cold are not the only irritations. In addition to drafts, one can distinctly hear voices speaking outside. Viewed as a shelter, the Japanese residence is something which is extremely humble, perhaps even incomplete. But for enduring the severe summer heat of Japan, it is good to have a structure which is open to outside air, or at least that is what is believed.

That may be one of the reasons why from ancient times the walls of a Japanese house have generally been extremely simple things. From the traditional *shinkabe* construction in which mud was smeared over bamboo strips, to the modern *okabe* construction in which lathing or plasterboard is finished with wainscoting or mortar, the wall is made of wood or bamboo or clay—materials found in nature. The Japanese wall allows the outdoors to be seen through cracks along the posts and beams, and it gives a hollow sound when tapped upon.

Of course the thick stone or brick walls of the homes in which many Westerners live are walls that provide very strong resistance. To a Westerner, a wall from the start is not a latticework pattern, but consists instead of tightly packed stone or brick or some similar material. Thus there is a huge gap between the western and Japanese concepts of a wall. I have personally inspected semi-detached duplex housing in a London suburb in which the thickness of the dividing wall was some 70 centimeters (27.5 inches). The residents told me that they could not

Traditional wall of plaster and wood (*shinkabe*).

Primitive example of *okabe* (clay and wood construction).

hear any noise from the neighboring house, even when someone was playing a piano right next to the common wall. These happened to be privately developed ready-built homes, but in fact in moderate-priced housing for the common people, no reduction in wall thickness is tolerated. I would say this is indicative of the tenacity of the western attitude toward the wall.

In German homes, which are mainly built of brick, the established standards generally call for exterior walls consisting of two layers of brick measuring about 49 centimeters (19.3 inches) in total thickness, and for interior dividing walls of a single layer measuring about 24 centimeters (9.5 inches). In Japan, recently built apartment buildings, even the finest ones, which are constructed of steel-reinforced concrete, have walls that are more or less 20 centimeters (7.9 inches) thick including woodwork, while *okabe* walls constructed of wood are about 15 centimeters (5.9 inches) thick *shinkabe* walls about six centimeters (2.4 inches) thick, and the walls of the traditional teahouse four centimeters (1.6 inches).

That being the case, I might add that in the European house the area upon which the walls sit is not considered part of the calculated floor area of the house, and the area of an interior wall is not included in the calculations of the area of the room. To calculate the area of the room, the measuring instrument is placed against the inner edge of the wall, and consequently the floor area is a true measure of the actual space of the room. But in Japan, that is not the case. According to the Japanese building code, the floor area of a building is "the projected horizontal area measured from the center lines of the walls or other partitions." Thus the thickness of the wall between its surface and its center line is included in the calculation of what is called the floor area of a room or building, while the usable floor area is somewhat smaller. The traditional Japanese system of measuring a room used lines connecting the center of one post to the center of another (the *shin-shin-hashira-ma* system). It came to be applied to walls as well, and ended up as a provision of the present-day building codes. The European method of measurement, called the "inside measure," is the sum of the areas of all of the rooms. It does not provide the total area of the house, since the area of the walls has to be added. The wall area can constitute up to 20 percent or more of the total area of the house, and in some cases the walls take up an area corresponding to one or two rooms of a house. Anyone who wishes to compare the areas of a western and a Japanese home, or to apply elements of one to the other, should keep this disparity in mind.

In western architecture, a wall is something which shuts out exterior heat, noise, light and air and at the same time protects the occupants from intruders. In Japan, the various functions a wall is expected to serve are much vaguer. In traditional reference works such as the *Daigenkai*, a famous dictionary, the meaning of a wall is given as an "architectural partition." Since sliding *shoji* and *fusuma* panels serve as spatial partitions, they are considered types of walls. This idea of the partition as wall seems to indicate the Japanese view of a "wall." However, the Japanese character which signifies wall (壁, *kabe*) is said to have originally meant "a fence of earth and stone erected to keep out an enemy." The Japanese character is derived from the Chinese, and this seems to be a Chinese interpretation of its meaning, for Chinese architecture, like European architecture, uses thick walls made from earth and stone. Proof of this can be found in another Chinese character (龕, *gan*), which is part of the Japanese language but is only very rarely used. The latter character is used to refer to decorative shelves built into a cavity that has been cut into a wall, upon which Buddhist images or the like may be displayed. It corresponds to the English "niche," referring to the area cut into a stone or brick wall in which statues of the saints may be placed. Such niches are often seen in churches and at town crossroads in Europe. There are no niches in Japanese architecture, and probably very few Japanese know the word for it in their own language.

The Japanese wall was at most a space partition and an interruption of the line of sight. The traditional Japanese wall is called a *shinkabe*; *shin* is probably derived from a word referring to the centers of the *hashira*, which it was designed to connect, as a thin, single-layer sheet. In western parlance, it might be called a "curtain" or a "curtain wall." In fact, it was a room divider, not a wall. When the character for wall came from China to Japan, it was given the Japanese pronunciation, *kabe*. The word created some confusion because in the Japanese living space there originally was nothing called a *kabe*. There were simply partitions. Ancient dictionary definitions support this view.

Considering that in Japanese architecture, with the exception of castles and storehouses, there traditionally was no such thing as a wall, it becomes a little easier to understand the perception of an outsider who labels Japanese homes which lack manmade environments enclosed by walls "austere." The real issue here is whether the Japanese will continue to carry on indefinitely with their austere, "wall-less" homes.

One reason Japanese homes do not have walls is that in order to en-

"Wall-less" Japanese house enclosed only by *shoji* (paper partitions).

dure the heat and humidity of summer, the house needs to be as open as possible. "A house should be built for summer. In winter one can live anywhere, but dwellings unsuited to the hot season are unbearable." These well-known words of the sage Yoshida Kenko (1283–1350) express a conviction that is still widely and firmly held. One might therefore expect that even partition-type walls, not to mention solid walls, are not often found in Japan. But that is not so. Although the homes of the nobility, in line with Yoshida's advice, were of very open design, the *machiya* townhouses and the commoners' farmhouses which developed from the pit dwelling had plenty of walls. Of course, these tended to be roughly constructed affairs daubed with mud; but rather than being of open design, these types of houses are fairly closed-in. An

important reason the nobility were able to have open-plan houses that could be partitioned at will was because they had high exterior walls surrounding their homes. The commoners, who could not afford such walls, had to enclose the interiors of their houses, even though the houses were meant to be "built for summer." The nobility owned a great deal of furniture and other household effects, but ordinary people who did not have much furniture relied on walls to install shelves and to hang things. All the same, it is probable that such walls were not at all comparable to the solid elements which are described as walls in China and Europe.

Among the houses of the nobility, in the *shinden* (palace) style of the Heian period (794–1185), there was something called *nurigome* used for bedrooms to meet demands to protect the room from the cold and to ensure privacy. Daubing the walls with earth to resemble a *nurigome* ("plaster cage") was a good way to do it.

Later, in the Edo period (1603–1867), townhouse styles appeared, called *nuriya-zukuri* ("plaster house style") and *kura-zukuri* ("storehouse style") which had thicker walls to help prevent fires. These townhouses can still be found throughout Japan. The inhabitants have not complained about any problems living in them. I once had the chance to visit the drawing room of an *igura* (a house of the latter style), and the owner assured me that it was cool in summer and warm in winter. Upon questioning it turned out that, oddly enough, the secret was in the ventilation. As a look at any Japanese storehouse will confirm, the storehouses were designed with careful attention given to good ventilation. Also, in order to decrease humidity, the ground beneath the floor was laboriously dug out to a depth of several meters and filled in with shells and sand. In the old days people attached great value to their possessions, and it seems that in some respects they gave greater consideration to the environmental quality of the storehouse, which held the all-important harvest, than to that of their homes. The well-closed-in space that resulted from that sort of concentrated effort is most assuredly a place that can be inhabited with ease.

Certainly Northern European homes need to be properly heated in winter, otherwise the buildings become so chilly as to be unlivable. Japanese winters, on the other hand, except on the northernmost island of Hokkaido, are mild compared with Northern European cold weather. In addition, the winter weather is clearer than that in Northern Europe, and buildings receive more sunlight. As long as the buildings or the rooms are not built facing north, where they will receive neither the morning nor the afternoon sun, they will not generally suffer from excessive chilliness.

It is not that the Japanese wall is absolutely not suited to Japanese circumstances; difficulties arise when ventilation and exposure to the sun are not considered. If careful attention is given to those areas, then the wall seems to be fairly appropriate to Japanese circumstances. The problem lies not necessarily with temperature but rather with humidity in the summer and light in the winter. The famous bone-chilling cold of Kyoto is caused by the humidity which is naturally found in its setting, a mountain-ringed basin that once contained a lake. Consequently, it is necessary to design and construct houses so as to remove humidity and to provide adequate ventilation and sunlight. When publicly sponsored apartment developments are completed and moisture condenses on the

Residential-cum-warehousing townhouses (*igura*). Merchandise is stored on the upper floor.

walls, causing mold to grow, they should be considered unlivable. The point is, these types of problems occur because holes for ventilation are not planned.

There are exceptions. There is an Italian woman who is married to a Japanese and living in Kyoto who, even at the height of summer, shuts all the doors in her house whenever it begins to rain and carries on with her daily routine. She says she does this to keep the house cool. And sure enough, upon entering the house, it seems slightly chilly. This is because the natural coolness of the morning is trapped inside the house. When we realize that cutting off ventilation also provides coolness, one begins to believe that the study of the modern Japanese home still has a long way to go.

Another method of maintaining the desired temperature and humidity is to invest in air conditioners or mechanical ventilation. This sort of technological solution may seem a bit distressing to purists, who are likely to be passionate humanists who pay no attention to material realities. Intensive research and planning toward the creation of living spaces which integrate science and technology in ways appropriate to the situation are required.

The Japanese people today are becoming a nation of critics on a cerebral level. Ever eager to increase the quantity of material goods in their own little niches, they remain unconcerned about the basic qualitative and functional poverty of the physical circumstances which surround them. Although they may possess the virtue of an austere spirit, it is a result of never really having known the taste of a material culture.

Doors

When people were still living in caves, they probably covered the cave entrances with stout rocks or logs in order to keep out hostile intruders. These obstructions served primarily as variations upon, or substitutions for, walls. It would also have been necessary to make a smallish opening in the upper part of the "wall" for lighting and ventilation. At this point, the cave, which had been enclosed by the wall, has come to require two sorts of openings: a covering and also an inlet. If the covering is regarded as a door and the inlet is regarded as a window, then we can understand how doors and windows are at the same time "walls" and "apertures." This is one way of viewing the basic difference between doors and windows.

Thus a door can be thought of as something which can be opened and closed; yet since the fundamental role is to shut out the outside world and to protect the interior environment, it could be called a "movable wall." In contrast, a window, which might be covered over by glass or by latticework or the like, is primarily something which faces out toward the exterior world, and can thus be regarded as an "aperture." We can use these terms with some validity to talk about the doors and windows of European and American houses. For example, the front door of a European or American house is likely to be a stout door made of oak or some other heavy wood, which might creak as it opens; at any rate it gives a feeling of substantiality. Normally the door is not glazed. In order to ascertain who is calling, there may be a peephole or a small window. The sort of glazed latticework that is commonly found on the main entrance of a Japanese house, which is regarded in a sense as stylish and in another sense as delicate, is not seen there. The same goes for the rear entrance.

In ancient times the doors of Japan were stout affairs. The

Fragile glazed *shoji* doors in a traditional farmhouse.

aristocratic residence from the Nara period (710–94) is known to us chiefly through the manor house of a Lady Tachibana, which was moved to the Horyuji Temple in Nara Prefecture and is now called the Dempodo. It is the oldest extant sample of Japanese residential architecture. This building is fitted with *itakarado* doors. Each of these magnificent doors is made from a single plank. The name, which transliterates from the Chinese ideographs as "T'ang board door," is indicative of the strong influence of Chinese architecture during the Nara period. In this type of architecture, the ancient Japanese *shitomido* (upward-swinging latticed shutters), like the contemporary *noren* (short curtains for doorways), were attached to the top of the entryway. Although entryways were protected by straw or rush matting in primitive times, this duty was by and large performed by wooden doors, at least in the houses of the affluent in the historical era. During the Heian period (794–1185), doors consisting of heavy wooden crosspieces mounted in a lattice pattern made their appearance. Although these had gaps in them, they were indeed worthy of being called doors, for they were so stout as to be virtually impossible to break down. The lower sections fitted together like a wall, a construction that prevented people from entering or leaving. Today the upper parts which opened outward to be attached to hooks on the underside of the roof overhang might be labeled "windows," but I would rather call them half-doors than windows.

Shinden-style building with upward-opening, latticed shutters (*shitomido*).
A reconstruction of far older forms. Kyoto Imperial Palace.

Rails at the edge of the veranda onto which sliding "doors" are placed.

The Japanese have long made the fundamental distinction between doors, which were the partitions separating the house from the outside, and *shoji*, the translucent sliding panels which separated the interior rooms. While Japanese doors were not the sort of devices that served as walls or entranceways as they did in the West, they did offer a sense of protection. From ancient times, shutting the door is referred to as *to o tateru* (literally, to set up or to erect the door). Likewise, the phrase *tatetsuke ga warui* refers to ill-fitting doors, but is based upon the same verb which means "to stand," since the doors were lifted onto rails and "stood" there. From the derivation of these words we can see that the door was regarded as a type of protection. In fact, even now there are many farmhouses that do not have permanently attached sliding doors or even storage bays into which the doors slide. Instead the wooden doors are carried from some other storage area each time they are required, and inserted between the lintels and doorsills of the outer wall.

The development of *garasudo* ("glass doors") has confused the function of the door with the window since the Japanese word is a combination of the English word "glass" and the Japanese word for door (*do*). Viewed through European eyes, such a flimsy, delicate construction might be considered a window designed to admit light, and not a door with the implied barrierlike function. The wooden *amado* shutter could be an example of what is meant in the West to be a door. But in Japan the doors that separate the veranda from the interior rooms are always called *garasudo*. Consequently, because of the shutters which are fitted on the outside, a veranda actually requires two sets of doors for each opening.

The glass door originated from the *shoji* (sliding paper doors). To admit more light, the paper of the *shoji* was changed to glass. To be precise it should not be called a "glass door" but rather a "glass *shoji*." However, for some reason we have come to call it a glass door. The *shoji,* as noted above, was developed as an interior partition. When it is used as an exterior partition, another set of doors becomes necessary. If the second set of doors is thought of as shutters, then, in terms of shelter, the Japanese house is complete. Actually the Japanese *amado* shutters prove the versatility of the Japanese house. They can be put quickly in place to keep out rain, dampness, etc., or they can be stored in a convenient place during pleasant weather, creating the open-style Japanese house. As far as the names are concerned, if they were called

Removable wooden *amado* shutters and storage bay into which the shutters can be hidden.

glass *shoji* and shutters, those names would be appropriate. On the other hand, if there were no shutters but only glass *shoji*, then as a shelter the Japanese house would seem incomplete.

Recently built houses do not have shutters. This may be because people think it quite enough to have a door, in the form of the "glass door." It is also accurate to state that architects, wishing to erect buildings as cheaply as possible, prefer to eliminate shutters and similar appurtenances when feasible. Some say that when the "glass door" consists of a modern aluminum frame, then shutters are no longer needed. And architects, who have been infected with westernism, dislike the *amado* and *tobukuro* designs and prefer not to use them.

Certainly in European and American homes, when there are no balconies, there usually are no shutters on the windows. Instead the glass used for the windows is rather thick. This is because the idea of glass being a "transparent wall" is becoming more and more widespread. Furthermore, in Northern Europe it is taken for granted that glass windows will be double-glazed. Most glass doors in Japan, by way of contrast, consist of a single layer of glass that is only two or three millimeters thick; after all, isn't a glass door really just the partition called a *shoji* in which glass has been substituted for paper? Thus it naturally is a structure which cannot effectively block out drafts, driving rain or noise. If thought is given to typhoons or intruders, or to leaving the house empty for a longish interval, then the extra layer of shutters becomes necessary. If there is no door, then the fundamental closing-up aspect of the house disappears.

A great many Japanese people live in houses that have no shutters. When the wind blows with any seriousness, they have to put up with a good deal of rattling and shaking. It is then that the contemporary Japanese house, caught between tradition and modernism, nervously confesses its own insecurity.

Windows

It might be an exaggeration to say that the window began to enter the lives of the Japanese when aluminum frames started to be used in average housing. But a Japanese female acquaintance who has lived abroad told me that even at times when she did not particularly enjoy the life there, she always had the "great pleasure of living with windows."

The window is generally understood to be an aperture cut into a wall for lighting and ventilation. Within the limits of that definition, there is not much difference between the Japanese window and the western window. But when it comes to how the windows are actually used, there is a great deal of difference between the two.

Look at the way a window provides lighting, for example. We usually think of the lighting function of a window solely in terms of the light coming in through the window. But another important function is *not* admitting light. A European window is often equipped with a blind or shutter to block out the light. Although traditional homes in Japan had *amado* shutters for use during storms, the mass-produced or contemporary homes do not even have these in most cases. Many people believe that architects, contractors and even administrative staff of public housing organizations require curtains on western-style windows. But if this were really true, then such windows would be fitted not only with curtain rods but also with valances, so that when the curtains are closed, exterior light would be completely prevented from entering the bedroom. This is not the case. Only a few of the people involved in building homes seem to realize that, by and large, for a living-room window, a rail for lacy daytime curtains and another rail for drapes for evening use are both necessary. In most Japanese residences, a curtain is simply something which is intended to block out direct sunlight or to prohibit outsiders from looking in. It is not considered a device which allows complete control over the brightness or darkness of a room.

When it comes to ventilation, there are also significant differences between the western window and the Japanese window. A western window, whatever its shape, can usually be opened. Thus, for ventilating purposes, a window is required to be freely movable and to be equipped to do so. The critic Michiko Inukai (1921–   ), who once lived in a German house, said she wanted to take a German window home to Japan as a souvenir. She contended that a German window was designed to aid ventilation in a number of ways: (1) to constantly ventilate without chilling the air in the room, (2) to let in light breezes, and (3) to change the air in the room when it is raining. Moreover, she was impressed that the German window could be opened completely.

Japanese windows, on the other hand, are constructed without much thought being given to such functions. The reason is that while ventilation of course is possible when the window is open, it is also possible for air to enter through cracks when it is shut. This might be pleasant enough in the summer, but when an icy wind comes whistling through in the middle of winter, it is not such a blessing. The traditional Japanese window could allow ventilation, but it could not prevent it, just as it can allow light in but is unable to keep it out. In other words, because the window is not airtight, precise control of ventilation is impossible. Moreover, the Japanese window is hopelessly unable to completely block out unpleasant sounds and smells, cold or heat, or rain or dust from the outside.

Looked at in this way, we realize that the windows of the majority of contemporary homes in Japan are simply light-admitting apertures, and they are not regulating devices like western windows, which are used to selectively admit or exclude various exterior stimuli.

Yet it is not necessarily correct to say that Japan, broadly speaking, is a country where the window has not yet fully developed. One may be tempted to explain the fact that the functions of the window are not complete by simply saying that it results from centuries of impoverishment. However, historically Japan has had a very large variety of windows. If we go to a temple or another traditional Japanese building, aside from rectangular windows we will often see such elaborate window forms as *marumado* (circular windows), *tanzakumado* (windows found in teahouses and *sukiya*-style houses* made from fine-quality writing paper) or *katomado* (ogee-arched windows). Moreover, in *sukiya*-style residences and traditional Japanese hotels there are various interesting windows ranging from *renjimado* (lattice windows), *musomado* (hit-and-miss win-

Circular window (*marumado*).

A sort of bay window (*demado*) partially obscured by bamboo slats.

Various decorative windows of the restaurant Sumiya, a lavish establishment dating from the Edo period.

An unplastered decorative aperture (*shitajimado*).

dows), *demado* (bay windows) and *shitajimado* (openings in a wall formed by leaving the framework unplastered) to types which take their names from their positions or functions, such as *tenmado* (skylights), *ranma* (transom windows), *hakidashimado* (windows through which sweepings are thrown out) or *shoinmado* (study windows). If we also count such elegant designs as the *hana-akarimado* (interior windows opening on to a corridor or other exterior space) and *yukimimado* (picture window), then the number seems limitless. Looking at these varieties of windows only, Japan appears to be a country in which the window has reached a very high stage of development.

The Japanese word for window, "*mado*," is said to derive from the words "*ma*" (space, room) and "*do*" (door). In the Nara period (710–94) the use of windows as conveyers of light for reading spread to Japan from China, where monks in Buddhist temples had developed them to read their sutras in dark temples. The Japanese used their own word *mado* as an alternative reading for the Chinese character. "*Ma*" has the meaning of "a space between two posts," as well as the second meaning of a room, and "*do*" implies a door between two posts as well as a door to a room; these meanings are not, however, very clear in either case. It is also possible that *ma* could have been a simple prefix, but in any event, it seems that until the Japanese adopted the Chinese character and concept which are now referred to as "*mado*," the Japanese regarded a window as a class of door.

A "study window" (*shoinmado*). Dojinsai, Togu-do, Jisho-ji. Late 15th century.

The earliest form of the Japanese window can perhaps be envisioned by looking at the *shitomido* (upward-swinging latticed shutters). It served many functions. Unlike the *hiki-chigai mado* (double-sliding windows) or *hiraki mado* (casement windows) which are commonly seen in contemporary Japan, the *shitomido* consists of a *shoji* which is pushed up and out and held open with a metal or wooden prop suspended from the eaves, a type of construction which today is called a *tsukiage-mado*. In ancient times, before paper, let alone glass, was in use, the *shitomido* was made of straw or planks. The *shitomido* was clearly a door to a shelter, or a "moving wall," yet when it was lifted up and opened, control of light and ventilation were added, and thus it became a type of window. In this case, it is relatively simple to control by suspending its weight from above. Although the *shitomido* is simply constructed, it is able to regulate light and ventilation. Moreover, it has the added advantage of serving, when opened upward, as a sort of canopy for protection against rain or sun. And when it is closed, it not only serves as a light shade, but it also closes up the space.

The desire to admit light developed as the Chinese literary culture grew in Japan. As a result, windows came primarily to serve not as a means of opening and closing a shelter but as devices to admit natural brightness in the form of sunlight into the dwelling in order to provide light for interior reading and writing. Of course, the ancient Japanese, overwhelmed by the advanced civilization of China, immediately embraced the window culture. This need spurred the invention of *washi* (Japanese paper). Japanese windows fitted with light-admitting *shoji*, as the novelist Jun'ichiro Tanizaki (1886–1965) has admiringly pointed out, created the unique Japanese interior space in which the distinction between light and shadow is somewhat vague, which, in turn, nurtured the *in'ei* (shadow) culture that has given a special character to the whole of Japanese culture.

In this way the Japanese window, influenced by the window reading developed in China, advanced further and became a cultural interior device which produced the *in'ei* space—the mystical, sensual world in which literature and logic were viewed in a shadowy light. The window then developed not so much as a device for improving living standards, but more as a decorative or artistic item. Some windows, such as the "boar's eye window" of Shogetsusai Teahouse in Kyoto and the octagonal window of Kohoan Teahouse at Daitokuji Temple in Kyoto, are considered works of art and have been given personal names.

Yet this characteristic of the Japanese window was mainly confined to the temple and *shoin*-style architecture of the ruling classes. Such in-

Latticed shutters (*shitomido*) suspended from the eaves by iron hooks.

Two variations of open plaster storehouse windows (*takamado*).

Plaster and lattice townhouse windows (*mushikomado*).

convenient and expensive items were never intended to be installed in the houses of the general public. In the houses of the common people, practical installations, such as the *shitomido*, remained in use. Of course there were a number of exceptions such as the high windows in storehouses, the plastered-and-latticed windows of townhouses, and the exposed-framework windows of teahouses. Moreover, the sets of two or four *shoji* or, in some cases, doors, which were and still are in common use to close off verandas, can be said to be the windows—providing light and ventilation—of the average person's house.

The window proper first appeared in the homes of common people only just prior to World War I, in the two-story homes of middle- and upper-class businessmen. The appearance of glass and the subsequent spread of its use contributed to the widespread adoption of western-style windows. However, if glass merely replaces *washi* paper in the wooden *shoji* frames, the windows tend to rattle continuously when the wind blows. As a result many people, even today, have not had the pleasure of being in a house with real windows. The introduction of the aluminum frame brought the first airtight windows to Japan and gave us our first taste of a lifestyle in which "sunbathing" was possible even in winter and lightweight clothes were sufficient indoors. In terms of the history of the Japanese window, this was a truly revolutionary development.

Although the aluminum frame made possible the airtightness which had not existed with previous wooden house fittings, not much consideration has been given to controlling ventilation and lighting. The provision of rails for screens in aluminum sashes was a step forward, but various problems still remained for storm windows or shutters. In addition, the natural color of aluminum seems aesthetically unsuited to the wooden buildings of Japan. Of course products to which color has been applied are also available at additional cost. In Northern Europe, research is being conducted to develop wooden sashes which will surpass metallic sashes both aesthetically and functionally. With this in mind it seems that that the "window culture" of the Japanese has reached the threshold of reform.

*Sukiya literally means "abode of refinement." General emphasis in this style, which emerged in the Edo period (1603–1867), was placed on individual use, personal likes and dislikes, and a relaxed atmosphere, in contrast to the more formal, public, and official features of the shoin style. As a result each sukiya-style building was unique, yet shared certain common characteristics, such as window, transom, and shelf forms.

Shoji

The Japanese are geniuses at miniaturizing anything. After the war, the transistor radio became synonymous with Japan. Today the Walkman and the laptop computer maintain the image. Japanese electric appliances, such as washing machines, refrigerators and televisions, are usually quite small, with all sorts of lilliputian models to choose from. Familiar items used daily, from cameras and automobiles down to clothespins and paper clips, tend to come in smaller sizes in Japan.

I once visited a dam on the Obi River in Siberia. One day, while our bus was racing at full speed across a giant plain that stretched as far as the eye could see, an announcement informed us that we had arrived at the dam. But looking around we could see no water, only the plain. When we complained, our interpreter replied that the Obi River was visible. We looked around again and realized that on both sides of us the horizon looked glitteringly bright. And indeed, we were smack in the middle of an earthen dam stretching several kilometers in width (not length). Although the Westerners aboard must have been impressed, the Japanese were astounded.

In Japan the trend to miniaturization is especially remarkable. For example the *tsubo* garden recreates in only one tsubo (3.3 square meters, or 35.5 square feet) a beautifully condensed scene which represents mountains and oceans. Interior architecture includes various established small spaces such as the tea ceremony room, which appeared during the Muromachi period (1333–1573), when the teamaster Takeno Jo-o (1502–55) designated the small four-and-a-half tatami-mat room as the standard. The tradition has been carried on by succeeding generations of tea masters. The space has been compressed successively to rooms of three-and-three-quarters mats, three mats, two-and-three-quarters mats, two mats and even one-and-three-quarters mats. (One mat is ap-

A typical *tsubo* (miniature) garden.

proximately 90 cm × 180 cm, or 2 feet 11 inches × 5 feet 11 inches.) Of course at that time the burning issues of contemporary Japan, the "land squeeze" and "housing scarcity," were not relevant. The amount of space was pared to the cramped minimum because the small space was thought to promote the world of *wabi* (calm simplicity), the central concept in the tea ceremony. This tea ceremony architecture crystallized into the *sukiya* style (see previous chapter), which to this day remains the basic traditional design parameter for the Japanese residence. Thus it is to this legacy that those who would curse the tininess of the Japanese house might well address themselves.

There is another structural peculiarity of Japanese material culture which coincides with miniaturization, and that is making things lightweight. At times, the combination of lightness with smallness can make our lives seem larger. We tend to sense this strongly when we go abroad or come into contact with foreign products. From coins, keys,

Exterior view of a teahouse. Manshuin Temple.

Interior view of the same teahouse.

doorknobs and coffee cups to chairs, beds and bath towels, it seems that whatever foreign item we touch gives us a weighty sensation which can be slightly disorienting. But if we think about it, most things Japanese are perhaps too light. Chopsticks are a perfect example. In contrast to the metallic weightiness of a knife or fork, Japanese chopsticks are always made of lightweight wood, or sometimes bamboo. In China, there are chopsticks made of silver or ivory, but in Japan there is no tradition of making chopsticks from such materials. When a Westerner looks at a picture of a Japanese breaking apart a pair of flimsy, disposable chopsticks and eating some delicate morsel, say a leaf bud, he is liable, with a little smile, to shake his head and wonder whether the Japanese might survive by eating air.

If chopsticks are the symbol of lightness in the realm of food, the sliding *shoji* panel, which is a cedar lattice with translucent paper stretched over it, is a similar symbol. It can easily be slid open with one finger along a sill that has mere two- or three-millimeter notches to hold the *shoji* in place. Foreigners are often amazed at the ease with which these large panels can be opened. In the West where most doors are of the hinged push-open type, there are sliding doors, but aside from the few that may be modeled after Japanese *shoji* and *fusuma* (opaque sliding screens), these are heavy affairs that rumble along their rails, making a noise that sounds like a minor earthquake. Usually it takes two people to remove one of these doors with any ease. Doors which slide apart or behind one another are sometimes known as ''sliding walls'' in English, and that is indeed an appropriate name for such devices.

Most of the rooms of a traditional Japanese house are separated by *shoji* or *fusuma*. A main advantage of these partitions is that they can all be easily removed to convert a whole floor of the house into a single large room. In former times, and in some places even today, a farm-house can be turned into a banquet hall on a ceremonial occasion by removing all the *shoji* and *fusuma*. This example points out that fundamentally the traditional Japanese home is a one-room house which has been partitioned into a series of compartments by the *shoji* and *fusuma*. This is the major characteristic of space allocation in the Japanese traditional house.

In most countries the house began as a single room. This was turned into the large and complex spaces which we know today by widening or multiplying the number of rooms and developing systems of dividing and connecting them. In European homes with stone or brick walls, there is a structural limit on the size of a room. When living requirements dictate that a wider space is necessary, the only way to pro-

Opaque sliding screens (*fusuma*; foreground).

vide it is to add on one or more entirely new rooms. The most primitive
method of connecting the rooms is to build a series of rooms right up
against each other with connecting doorways between them so that each
room doubles as a passageway, as in the "labyrinth house" style found
in the ancient Far East or in such ancient Greek cities as Troy or Crete.
In large-scale European structures such as the 18th-century Palace of
Versailles, the method of connecting rooms was really no different. The
dominant house pattern in ancient Rome was to arrange all the rooms
around an atrium which provided passage among them. This pattern
survives today in Southern Europe in homes in which each room opens
onto a central garden or patio. In China such a courtyard style, in
which the surrounding building is divided into homes for small families,
each consisting of one room and a door, is common.

But the Japanese house has developed entirely differently. That is, a single room can be extended in size. In contrast to the western or Chinese house to which rooms of similar size were added on in succession, as in a honeycomb, the Japanese house retains its single room and inflates it when necessary, rather like blowing up a balloon. House design based on such a pattern, which seems to have originated in the four-square-grid-style samurai houses of the Kamakura period (1185–1333), was consummated as an established architectural style in the *shoin* (writing hall) style of the Muromachi period. This style was characterized by a decorative alcove, staggered shelves, a built-in desk and decorative doors, although rarely were all these features found in a single *shoin* dwelling.

Previously the homes of the ruling class were in the *shinden*, or palace, style which had been established several centuries earlier in the Heian period (794–1185). Modeled after Chinese palace architecture, this style contained a main chamber (the *shinden* or *seiden*) and one or more out-buildings (called *tainoya*) situated to the east, west or north. They were connected by corridors in what might be called a chainlike configuration. Each of the buildings in the *shinden-tainoya* series contained a main room surrounded by verandas. This concentric planar structure was not interrupted by partitions between the central room and the verandas. The only partitions were hinged shutters (*shitomido*) or doors (*tsumado*) along the exterior of the verandas. Thus each of the constituent buildings consisted of a single room and a single roof, that is they were one-room dwellings. Enlargements of these buildings were carried out in a pattern of concentric construction, which would eventually reach a limit. It is possible to think of the *shinden* style as being the ancient Japanese Shinto shrine buildings which were one-room, one-roof buildings. Later influenced by the Chinese style, they stretched around a garden in a bisymmetrical pattern. Before *shoji* came into use, the various shrine buildings, especially the core building, were a fixed size and could not become larger. In addition, these buildings were generally quite dark as there were few devices for allowing light to enter.

But the samurai houses, which appeared during the Kamakura and Muromachi periods, brought an end to nobility's strict ultraconservative adherence to the tradition of the T'ang Chinese/ancient Japanese bisymmetrical building arrangement with its concentrically structured interiors. I believe this movement was supported by new construction technologies, namely the appearance of the square pillar (*kakubashira*) and the development of paper-covered *shoji*.

Shinden-style complex with its interconnected buildings. Kyoto Imperial Palace.

Main chamber of the Kyoto Imperial Palace.

It may be a slight exaggeration to speak of the "appearance" of the square pillar, but until that time round pillars were the general rule. One reason for this was that construction tools were not highly developed. A second factor was connected to the Japanese acceptance of the Chinese canon of "round heaven, square earth." Since the pillar was connected to the ceiling (heaven), it had to be round according to the belief. The problem was that a purely cylindrical pillar, which could only be made from a squared-off log, was expensive and difficult to obtain in sufficiently large sizes. Therefore square pillars began to be used more widely.

During the era of round pillars, such interior furnishings as reed mats, *kicho* curtains (curtains on moveable T-frames) or folding screens, were generally placed between the lined-up pillars to partition the main rooms from the verandas. When square pillars came into use, lintels and sills were fitted to them, and it became possible to install sliding *shoji* rather simply, using the square pillars as door frames. Sliding is the most convenient way of opening and closing *shoji*. There are sliding doors in many countries, but the use of a partition, in which two or four doors slide behind one another on a pair of grooves in the sill, is something which is thoroughly Japanese. Paper played a very large role in the development and diffusion of *shoji* in Japan.

Shoji themselves did not exist in the Nara period (710–94) but first appeared during the Heian period. In the beginning boards were used as dividers. Then thick, heavy, non-lucent paper was added, creating what came to be called the *fusuma*. With the development of *akari shoji* (the contemporary *shoji* with translucent *washi* paper stretched across a grid of thin wooden crosspieces) the Japanese interior space acquired its characteristic of being able to expand without limit. In other words, *fusuma* and *shoji*, due to their lightness, can be smoothly opened and closed without disturbing the air in the room, while also serving as room dividers. Moreover, transoms above the *fusuma* and/or the translucent paper of the *shoji* allow the diffusion of natural exterior light into the room.

A Westerner, hearing that Japanese homes are made of wood and paper, is likely to imagine some flimsy little structure. Imagine, however, his surprise if he were to see the gigantic "single-room spaces" of *shoin* architecture, which, thanks to the paper, can be large halls comprising some tens or even hundreds of tatami mats (each measuring about 2 square meters, or 21.4 square feet). The Katsura Palace, the villa of the Katsura-no-miya line of princes in Kyoto, is one of the finest masterpieces of the Japanese "single-room space" culture. It is interesting that Japanese architecture has managed to create a "wall" from a single layer of paper in a country which lies in the monsoon belt.

And the pursuit of lightness in Japanese architecture today is being enhanced by the development of sophisticated, lightweight aluminum and plastic building materials. It is not surprising that these construction materials have caught on with remarkable speed in a nation with such an ingrained tradition of the lightweight. This acceptance may be more than mere convenience, for a nation in which paper was the basis of "single-space" architecture. It remains to be seen what sort of architecture will emerge in Japan next. This is something which will be watched with great interest.

An example of expanded space obtained by removing partitions between pillars. Note the elevated tatami floor in the background (*jodan-no-ma*) on which those of higher status sat. Audience Hall of Nishi Hongan-ji Temple, rebuilt early 17th century, in Kyoto.

Katsura Detached Palace (early 17th century), in Kyoto, a harmonious
blend of inside and out.

Floors

The historian Arnold Toynbee (1889–1975) was invited to a home during his visit to Japan. In the entryway he was politely reminded that local custom demanded that he remove his shoes, and he reports that he felt a bit embarrassed.

The custom of not wearing shoes inside the house is found, aside from Japan, only in a few other Asian countries. Thus a lifestyle of distinguishing between "upper" and "lower" floors, which has been second nature to the Japanese since ancient times, is in global terms quite rare. What embarrassed Toynbee was the realization of how unclean it really is, from the point of view of the western rationalist spirit, to come in from the dirty outside world and wear the same shoes all the way into the bedroom—and enduring at the same time the realization of how barbaric western culture has been to persist for centuries in just such a form of behavior.

That comes from the professor's own reminiscences. One might be tempted to argue that since all the streets in Europe are paved, perhaps one's shoes are not so dirty that they can't be worn into the house. Perhaps it is only a question of degree, since the amount of garbage or dust on the street doesn't change so much from country to country. The travel diaries of missionaries who visited Japan during various eras are unanimous in noting with admiration how Japanese streets were kept scrupulously clean and rinsed with water. Considering that until about one hundred years ago garbage and offal were thrown into the street from the homes in Europe and that packs of dogs and pigs picked through it, the missionaries were undoubtedly impressed with the well-kept Japanese streets.

The Japanese *yuka* (floor), which developed as a result of this custom of removing the shoes, represents a "dwelling culture" which is

Entrance to lavish Edo-period restaurant Sumiya. Note: patrons removed
their shoes on the stone step before entering the building.

unique. The *yuka* is certainly not equivalent to what is called a floor in English. On a floor, street shoes are permitted; on the *yuka* they are strictly forbidden. The only acceptable English term would be "raised floor."

Looked at developmentally, this raised floor is part of the tradition of a raised-floor architecture which comes from Southeast Asia. It originated as a result of a need to maintain sanitary, healthy conditions despite monsoon flooding and general dampness. In Laos, for example, to this day a distinction is made between the polluted world below floor level and the unpolluted world above it. The area beneath the floor is used only for storage or to house animals.

Because the Japanese relied on rice cultivation, Japanese communities were established largely in the wet regions around river deltas. Consequently, the Japanese gradually shifted from the pit dwellings which developed in the north during the Jomon period (10,000 B.C.–300 B.C.) to the raised-floor architectural style which was adopted in the south and took root there during the Yayoi period (300 B.C.–A.D. 300).

Yet it wasn't simply a case of progression from the pit dwelling to the raised-floor dwelling. From depictions of the buildings of the time on ceramic objects, bronze bells and mirrors it can be surmised that the storehouses were the first structures to be built in the raised-floor fashion since these structures were all-important to the farmer. Next, shrine buildings and the homes of the nobility were changed to the raised-floor style. For a long period, the common farmers' homes remained similar to pit dwellings, with earthen floors covered with straw or rice husks. There were no wooden floors such as are seen today. During the Edo period (1603–1867) some farmhouses began to have wooden floors, but even then earthen floors were still the norm in the agricultural villages of Tohoku, Shinshu and other regions in the northern part of Honshu Island. Indeed, most people living in villages did not have proper floors (*yuka*) until after the Meiji Restoration of 1868. In the towns, the *yuka* became the basic floor design only in the modern era. Before that the townhouses, like farmhouses, had earthen floors covered with straw. For a long time the *yuka* was used exclusively in the homes of the privileged classes: the nobility, the clergy and the samurai.

Thus the raised floor of the Japanese home is something which is quite old in historical terms, but it is not so old in terms of its spread among the common people. It is surprising that more than a thousand years were to pass between the adoption of the floor in the everyday life of the nobility and its diffusion among the population in general. Once the *yuka* had been introduced, it became an integral part of daily life.

A third-century Japanese bronze mirror depicting the four basic architectural types: raised storehouse, raised dwelling, ground-level structure and pit dwelling.

A reconstructed pit dwelling. Toro Park, Shizuoka Prefecture.

A reconstructed raised storehouse. Toro Park, Shizuoka Prefecture.

The Japanese, regardless of how westernized they are, do not give up their customs of removing their shoes when entering the house and sitting on the floor. Even in a western-style hotel, the fastidiousness with which the Japanese insist upon removing their shoes and putting on slippers seems to indicate a permanent attachment to this custom.

As for modern homes, Japanese often complain that the raised-floor space, which is supposed to be very sanitary, retains dampness. In particular, people say that one should be careful not to place valued clothing in closets on the north side of the house. And there are many homes where clothing placed in the lower drawers of a dresser is especially vulnerable to mildew. In order to avoid the problems of their damp climate, the Japanese made the switch from pit dwellings to raised-floor dwellings, so why are they still suffering from the effects of dampness?

One reason seems to be related to the construction of contemporary homes. During the past century, the great Tokyo earthquake of 1923 brought major changes to the Japanese wooden home. Many structures in the area collapsed during the earthquake because the wooden homes had weak footings. Typically, while the upper structure remained intact, as the pillars and groundwork were suddenly jolted the short posts supporting the ground-sill fell sideways, weakening the structural frame, and as a result the whole house caved in. The remedy for this problem turned out to be the real cause for the dampness people suffer in their homes today. Previously, private homes had been built around a heavy central pillar, known as the *daikokubashira*, which rested securely on a foundation stone partially embedded in the ground. Gradually the central pillar was replaced by a series of thin posts which supported the lower floor of the house. It was this new building method that was the problem in the earthquake. Consequently, new construction techniques were quickly adopted in which the short posts which had been supporting the lower floor were eliminated. Instead a concrete slab foundation, usually about 30 centimeters (11.8 inches) deep, was poured and the flooring was affixed to it with bolts. Small ventilation ports covered with metal mesh to deter mice were inserted in the concrete.

This technique did effectively stabilize the structure of the house, but the ventilation, having been largely blocked off by the poured-concrete foundation, was no longer sufficient. Of course, the concrete foundation has eliminated the openness seen, for example, in the short posts under the floor of the main hall of a traditional temple. Furthermore, in recent years not enough attention has been given to ventilation. For some inexcusable reason the ventilation holes in the concrete have tended to become smaller as well as fewer. One even comes across homes that do not have any at all. By erecting concrete walls as well, which are functionally equivalent to earth in terms of construction techniques, we have reverted to the pit dwelling. We might say we have a pit dwelling with a floor. But the special precautions are missing which were taken in the case of the pit dwelling: selecting a site with a relatively low moisture level and baking the earthen floor dry.

It is not my intent to criticize the poured-concrete foundations. They have not only improved housing construction but have also increased security against intruders. But we must remember that Japan is one of the few countries in the world in which the home has evolved from the raised floor. Having inherited the tradition of the raised-floor home, we need to make a serious effort to use it in the construction of contemporary housing, or we will lose the merits of this excellent tradition.

Nowadays, the custom of a major annual housecleaning is being abandoned. In the old days this involved taking up the tatami mats, removing the floorboards, drying out the area under the floor and making a general inspection. As most people today do not have enough time for this kind of house maintenance, it is necessary to give some thought to devices which can prevent moisture from accumulating under the floor or provide continual ventilation. This can be accomplished by providing ditches or berms around the foundation to prevent water from flowing from the earth underneath the floor, or by opening a large hole for ventilation, aligned with the prevailing wind direction. Such measures are necessary in order to make the *yuka*, which so impressed Professor Toynbee, a more agreeable living space.

Westerners prefer to wear their shoes indoors, feeling that the shoes are part of one's outer garments and that it is impolite to remove them. This is probably a result of the need to keep the feet warm on cold floors which are made of hard materials such as stone or cement. On the other hand, because flooring materials in Japan provide insulation and prevent dampness, they permit the Japanese to follow their custom. It is conceivable that in the future we could see the adoption of this Japanese dwelling custom elsewhere. In at least one elementary school in America the children go barefoot both indoors and out, for it is thought by some that this is healthier than wearing shoes. If that is true, then perhaps the Japanese custom should not be discarded.

Tatami Mats

Once while I was participating in a roundtable discussion on housing, I commented, ''These days, the housing consciousness of the Japanese seems to be decreasing''—to which a newspaper editor immediately responded, ''The Japanese have had a very strong housing consciousness since ancient times, and I believe that is still a part of our national heritage.'' Yet, I believe that whatever may have been true in the past, the housing consciousness among Japanese today is quite low.

In the past, for example, there were many people who, simply as a hobby, were more knowledgeable than carpenters about such things as the proper way of putting together a sitting room or the correct procedure for selecting wood for paneling. And what do we find now? The youth of today, may know in detail for example, the body lengths and widths of all the latest automobile models, but how much do they know or care about the fact that the dimensions of the tatami mat have gradually been greatly trimmed?

Although tatami mat dimensions do not by themselves constitute the measurements for a dwelling, it is true that for many centuries the Japanese house has been standardized in terms of the number of mats per room and their dimensions. The sizes of rooms, pillars and lintels as well as the distances between pillars have been determined by the number and size of the tatami. Consequently, the dimensions of the tatami in the Japanese house are directly connected with the prescribed size of the space which constitutes the dwelling.

In former times, tatami mat sizes were generally fixed. Before World War II, there were three standard widths: the new *Kyoma* (Kyoto room) tatami was 95.5 centimeters, or 3 feet 2 inches (the old one had been 98.5 centimeters, or 3 feet 3 inches); the medium-size *Kyoma* tatami was 91 centimeters, or 3 feet; and the *inakama* (countryside room) or *Edoma*

(*Tokyo room*) tatami was 88 centimeters, or 2 feet 10 inches, wide. But since the war, the Japanese home has become smaller at a rate that is visible to any observer. Along with the appearance of publicly subsidized housing developments of steel-reinforced concrete construction, came tatami mats with widths in the neighborhood of 80 centimeters, or 2 feet 7.6 inches; and in some of the newer privately developed wooden structures a 70-centimeter, or 2 foot 3.6 inch version, known as *bunka* tatami or super-small-size tatami, has been installed.

In the contemporary small dwelling, the fact that the home has become smaller implies that domestic life has been compressed, thus oppressed. One of the tragedies of modern housing is that as possessions pile up inside the home, the actual living space for the occupants becomes smaller and smaller.

The tatami is a unique flooring material which developed only in Japan. Indeed, it is to some minds a symbol for all things Japanese. I have heard that among some French Japanophiles, highly proficient speakers of Japanese are called "tatamisers."

The tatami is a modular type of matting which can be used to cover a floor and can be used for sitting upon as well as sleeping on. Its existence is related to the virtual lack of chairs and beds in the Japanese living environment.

All over the world primitive dwellings, with the rather limited exception of tree houses, had earthen floors. Japanese primitive homes were no exception, although from an early date straw or rice husks were spread on top of the floor in the pit dwellings for sitting and sleeping purposes. In other words, the Japanese lived for centuries on earthen floors which were covered over with straw or husks. In fact, until rather recently Japanese farmhouses still had such floors.

In raised-floor houses, the planks of the floor were covered over with thin mats of plant fiber, animal skin or cloth. In the *Kojiki*, the oldest extant chronicle of Japan, it is recorded that the legendary emperor Jimmu sang the following song upon seeing his future empress, Isuzu Himenomikoto:

> In a hut
> In a field of reeds
> Sedge mats shall be spread
> And we shall sleep as one

This is typical of the ingenuous sentiment of the ancient era.

Thus, spreading something on top of an earthen or other type of floor is a very old custom in Japanese life. The tatami mat is one of the items

Round sitting mats scattered on tatami around a sunken hearth.

which was spread out and so used. The word originates from the Japanese verb *tatamu* (to fold), expressing the nuance of something which is folded over and stacked up. Since sedge and other plant fibers were used as floor coverings which could be spread out and folded up, these coverings developed into a type of mat.

When active interaction with the Asian mainland began in the 5th and 6th centuries, chairs and other devices for sitting, including a type of folding stool called the *agura*, were also introduced, but for some reason these did not become popular. Instead a thick, round cushion called the *warouda*, made of reeds woven together and suitable for use on the planks of a raised-floor house, came into widespread use. Beds had been introduced from the mainland during the Kofun period (the end of 4th century A.D. to the end of the 7th century). Ancient chronicles mention wooden and bamboo structures on the floors on which straw, mats or cloth would be spread. Since the name was usually appended to a prefix indicating a person of exalted status, these seem to have been used exclusively among the nobility. Meanwhile, we must suppose that the common man covered himself up in straw matting spread in a corner of the room. The *newara* (straw litters) which were still used by farmers of northeastern and west-central Japan in the latter part of the 19th century were probably the last of such arrangements.

What we call tatami today first appeared during the Heian period (794–1185) in *shinden*-style rooms, taking on the multiple roles of chair, cushion, bed and stool. Called *okitatami*, they were used as throw mats and spread in various parts of the room as the situation demanded. Similar to the tatami that we know today, these were rectangular with dimensions of about 180 by 90 centimeters (5 feet 11 inches by 2 feet 11 inches). From their shape and size, which seem to be based on the measurements of the human body, one would assume that these were beds, and indeed they were: various painted scrolls from the era depict people sleeping on them. Today a *chodai*, a canopied tatami bed, can still be seen in the Shishinden of the Kyoto Imperial Palace.

The shift from *okitatami* mats which were placed here or there in the room to the tatami mats which completely covered the floor of the room originated in the 15th century *shoin*-style homes of the samurai. This

A scroll painting showing aristocrats and priests seated on *okitatami* (throw mats) for a poetry gathering. Note the hanging scroll and potted plants in the background, a common method of display before the development of the alcove. *Bokiekotoba*, 1351.

probably occurred because of the relative ease and added convenience of laying the mats together in combination. The tatami mats at this point—modular and rectangular, with length and width in a two-to-one ratio—seemed to have returned to the configuration of the sedge mats which were in use some two millennia earlier.

With this combination of three basic functions—as a bed of standardized dimensions, as a cushion for sitting and as a covering for the entire floor—the tatami room reached completion. Later it was widely diffused and has survived to the present day.

According to the old Japanese saying *Tatte hanjo, nete ichijo,* or "Half a mat to stand, one mat to sleep," the size of the tatami mat was originally standardized as a bed, that is the mat was expected to match the dimensions of the human body.

Why shouldn't the tatami once again match the size of the body and be established in a social role? Doing so would reverse the trend to shrink room sizes, which, of course, depend on the tatami dimensions, and, in turn, this might help check the decline in the standard of living. Government statistics on housing size are still based on the number of tatami mats, without giving any official standard for the dimensions of the basic tatami mat. With the appearance of mats as narrow as the 70-centimeter- (2-foot-3-inch) wide tatami mat, such tallies become misleading.

Now is the time to clearly specify standards for tatami mat size. In plans for government buildings, the numerical values of 90 centimeters (2 feet 11 inches) by 180 centimeters (5 feet 11 inches) have often been adopted for tatami specifications. These figures were determined (with some slight rounding off) by substituting metric measure for the traditional carpentry standard of three by six *shaku.* In 1959, Japan formally abandoned the *shaku* measure in favor of metric measure. Indeed the 90-centimeter width seems to be a progressive step in comparison to the 80- (2-foot-7-inch) and 70-centimeter (2-foot-3-inch) widths, but a problem still remains. The Japanese have become remarkably taller in the postwar era.

Professor Nagayo Mochizuki, an architect and researcher on linear measure, has estimated that in ancient times the average height of an adult Japanese was five *shaku,* which is about 150 centimeters (five feet). Naturally it is rather difficult for us to calculate their actual heights. According to surveys carried out during the Meiji period (1868–1912), however, the average height for men was about 159 centimeters (5 feet 2 inches) and that for women 146 centimeters (4 feet 9.5 inches), for a combined average height of about 151 centimeters (4 feet 11.5 inches). This is a good point of reference. This figure increased somewhat during the years before World War II, but in the postwar period the average height of the Japanese grew quite rapidly, to more than 160 centimeters (5 feet 3 inches). By 1987, the average 17-year-old boy had grown to 170 centimeters (5 feet 7 inches) and the average 17-year-old girl had reached 158 centimeters (5 feet 2.3 inches).

In ancient times, when the height of the average person was about five *shaku*, the Japanese allowed for some variation, and made their tatami mats six *shaku* long. Similarly, taking the postwar average height as 160 centimeters (5 feet 3 inches) and increasing that by a margin of one fifth, the corresponding tatami size would be 192 centimeters (6 feet 3.5 inches) long by 96 centimeters (3 feet 2 inches) wide. This is almost precisely the size of a *Kyoma* (Kyoto room) tatami mat. Since the average height of the Japanese is now about 165 centimeters, then a tatami mat measuring about two meters (6 feet 7 inches) by one meter (3 feet 3 inches) is called for. Beds which are marketed today tend to be about that size; thus if a tatami is thought of as a bed, this is certainly not an unreasonable figure.

Now that the conversion from *shaku* to metric measure has been completed, it is an appropriate time to take into consideration the increase in the height of the Japanese and to establish tatami of roughly such dimensions as a societal standard from now on. Since tatami regulates the size of the Japanese home, it is one of its most important elements. Furthermore, it serves multifaceted purposes in the lives of the Japanese as a floor covering, a seat and a sleeping place. After all, as Japan achieves ever more impressive economic growth, it is only natural that we consider the growth of our living space as well.

Alcoves

The alcove, known as the *tokonoma* in Japanese, is an indispensable element of the Japanese sitting room. It functions as the only area designated for showing things in the traditional Japanese room, which is virtually devoid of decoration. The alcove is normally fitted with the requisite *tokobashira* (alcove post) and a few shelves arrayed in a staggered pattern, as well as a hanging scroll, an artistic ornament or a flower arrangement. The guest is seated near the alcove, but as etiquette demands that a guest who is invited into the sitting room be seated as close as possible to the alcove, which is a position of status or respect, the guest inevitably is seated with his or her back to it. This makes it impossible for the guest to fully appreciate the pains taken by the master of the house in constructing the alcove. It also inhibits appreciating the skill involved in selecting a certain ornament or scroll for the occasion from a collection which the host has likely built up over many years, or to enjoy the form of the flower arrangement which the hostess may have painstakingly created earlier in the day. It is normally the host and hostess themselves who, after having prepared the alcove for the occasion, are seated directly facing it.

Although the alcove is in the room which is used to receive guests, the question certainly arises as to just whose "appreciation space" it really is. If the alcove has such a tradition of usage and is supposedly the very essence of the household, then it would appear that the culture of the Japanese home is filled with paradox. This makes one wonder if the alcove, considering its purpose and the orientation of the host to the guests, is truly an ancient tradition of the culture of the Japanese house handed down from generation to generation. And is it really such an important space that it should be considered the core of the household?

Originally, the house took shape as the place where people could put their most valuable things. The Chinese (and Japanese) character for "house" (家) is composed of the radical signifying "roof" (宀) over the character for "pig" (豕). This would suggest that in ancient China, because pigs were food resources, they were prized possessions.

Now let us take a look at the prized possessions the Japanese traditionally kept inside their homes.

From the decoration on an extant bronze mirror of the 3rd or 4th century, we can surmise the shapes of dwellings at that time. It includes representations of four types of structures: raised-floor non-residential buildings, raised-floor dwellings, ground-level dwellings and pit dwellings. The most splendid among them was the raised-floor non-residential building with *chigi* (ornamented projecting rafter ends). Unlike the latter three buildings, which were actually used as people's homes, the first building was a storehouse. Naturally, the storehouse was regarded as more important than the home since in those days people's lives depended almost entirely on the amount of food they could preserve.

Later, as the social sphere was enlarged from the village to the nation and social stratification developed, these gabled-roofed raised-floor buildings became the sanctuaries of the gods, who were the spiritual rulers of the people, and the palaces of the kings, who were the temporal rulers of the people. They became what is known as shrine architecture. The most brilliant structures of the time, according to the illustrations in the ancient *Kojiki* and *Nihonshoki* chronicles, were those which were associated with consecration or enshrinement rites. (The *Kojiki* and *Nihonshoki*, which were compiled in the 7th and 8th centuries, chronicled Japanese history from mythical times to the 7th century A.D.) Objects which were believed to hold the spirits of the deities and other sacred royal relics were enshrined in these sanctuaries and palaces. According to the ancient chronicles of visitors from China who recorded the activities of the Japanese of that time, such embodiments or relics often took the forms of swords or of bows and arrows. There is an account in the *Kojiki* of how the legendary Emperor Jimmu, evading the fierce attack of his enemy Nagasunehiko, escaped to Kumano, Wakayama Prefecture, where he bored a hole in the ridge of a stout, high storehouse through which the sacred sword owned by the god Takemikazuchi-no-kami came down. This mythical event symbolizes the deep interconnection between the imperial throne of the emperor Jimmu and the stout, tall storehouses, similar in design to the *shinden*-style shrine (see chapter 6).

In the Asuka (593–710) and Nara (710–94) periods came the golden age of Buddhism. Influential nobles during these periods installed Bud-

A formal alcove (*tokonoma*) in the *shoin* style, with *shoin* window, scroll paintings, stand for *ikebana* flower arrangement or art object, and staggered shelf in the neighboring space.

dhist altars (*butsuden*) as the central points of their homes. It can be presumed that morning and evening devotions at these altars were obligatory.

During the ensuing Heian period (794–1185), the aristocracy of the theocratic state became fully formed. This meant that government affairs were conducted as ceremony, with people assembling in the *shinden*, or the main house, of the noble family's compound. This compound came to be called the *seiden*, or state chamber, where various ceremonies were carried out. Until then the most valued items in the house were food provisions or weapons, deified Shinto objects or Buddhist statues—in short, things rather than people, which at this point finally became the means of "interpersonal communication." This value system remained intact and influenced the *shoin* style of the following era, leading to the development of drawing rooms or meeting places, which functioned as reception areas, and ultimately to large-scale reception halls.

It was also the *shoin* style which ushered in the alcove. It is believed that this style developed in two ways. According to one belief, the alcove came into existence because the classification or division of rooms became blurred when people began to use tatami mats to cover the entire floor. Until that time throw mats (*okitatami*) had been in use, and a seating protocol (*suwariwake*) had evolved by which the number of mats on which a noble sat, or the color of the edging of the mat, was connected to his rank and social standing. When the room became uniformly covered with tatami such status distinctions disappeared. Then an architecturally defined area of piled-up tatami, basically a space with the floor raised a level higher than the main tatami room, was created.

The other view is that at the time a great many Sung (960–1277) and Yüan (1260–1368) dynasty hanging scrolls were imported from China. In the buildings of the preceding *shinden* style, paintings were done on partitions such as walls and sliding doors. In order to display this new type of art, which included Buddhist paintings displayed in scroll form (see page 81), an indentation was made in the wall and some thick planks were inserted into it.

The two generative lines of descent are, in meaning and character, completely different. On the one hand, the alcove is a raised area with significance as a "status space," and on the other it is a "showing space." In the later homes of the samurai, the alcove was wholly a display space. For example, it is said that in the alcoves of the senior retainers of the shogun in Edo (now Tokyo), a scroll was hung on the anniversary of the death of Tokugawa Ieyasu (1542–1616) and a festival

An early example of *tokonoma* in a farmhouse.

was held. In the tea ceremony rooms of the ordinary city dwellers, the alcove developed as a space for aesthetic appreciation. In those tea ceremony rooms (and this is true to this day) the guest was normally expected to be quite careful never to be seated with his or her back to the alcove. Thus the alcove originated from two different sources and later developed along separate lines in parallel fashion.

And what about the commoners' homes? From ancient times the focal point of the home of a commoner was the fire, that is the hearth or range. This held true for quite a long time. During that time it was important to receive guests and not to ignore them. The cultural anthropologist Naomichi Ishige (1937–) has pointed out that the basic difference between an animal's lair and a person's house is whether others of one's breed are invited into one's own space or not. In that sense reception spaces can be seen in any commoner's home of any era. In the 19th and early to 20th centuries, guests were shown to the guest rooms of farmhouses and to the sitting rooms of townhouses. But these rooms fell far short of being the most important spaces in the house, as with the earlier ruling and samurai classes. Instead, after a family had

Various types of folding screens on display. Gion Festival, Kyoto.

achieved a bit of comfort in their lives, the most important space in the common house was likely to be the storehouse or the Buddhist altar. In the event of a crisis such as a fire, people would rush first to guard the storehouses rather than the homes. When it came to saving personal property during a fire or other disaster, the choice was phrased as "the house or the altar." Many of the larger homes were centered around Buddhist family chapels. Until the late 19th century there were no alcoves in typical farmhouses or townhouses. When they did exist, they were separately provided appendages. To this day in Kyoto townhouses, the family treasure is not the hanging scroll or other artwork in the alcove, but the screens, which are shut away in the storehouse. The custom, which still prevails among tradesmen's homes in Kyoto, is to place such screens in the house for public viewing once each year during a special scroll-display festival.

The reception space of the common home took a major step forward at the time of the Meiji Restoration of 1868 when the shogunate lost control of the country and class distinctions weakened. In every home, a sitting room or a parlor of the sort that would be seen in an opulent residence was either assiduously installed, or at least was considered ideal. In those sitting rooms a special post (*tokobashira*), a rail (*tokogamachi*) and a reading desk with staggered shelves would be constructed. This room would be decorated with a hanging scroll painting of the emperor Meiji or of the sun goddess, or else it would be embellished with various artistic objects such as bamboo baskets or ceramic vases with flower arrangements. The choice of the scroll painting of the emperor or the picture of the sun goddess, was rather symbolic of the patriarchal authority which lay behind modern nationalism, and the choice of flowers or other artistic objects indicated the modern diffusion of high culture among the masses. In the end, the alcove, which we now envision as an overlap of a ''status space'' and a ''showing space,'' was shaped by the post-Meiji development of the common home.

Since the alcove had become a symbol of the fanatical paternalistic nationalism of the prewar years, the popularity of the alcove as a place to display scrolls or flower arrangements dwindled during the years of the postwar movement for democratization. In farmhouses, the electric fan became the ''treasure of the house'' to grace the alcove, and in new apartments, the alcove began to disappear altogether. This fate may have been inevitable, considering the fact that when the alcoves became popular in the Meiji era (1868–1912), most people did not possess hanging scrolls of the sort that should be hung there anyway.

Nowadays, many Japanese homeowners, having attained a certain affluence, are coming back around to a nostalgic feeling that, after all, a sitting room just isn't complete without an alcove and that it would be a nice thing to have.

Earthen Floors

The earthen-floored room has virtually disappeared from the Japanese house today. The concrete floor of the vestibule or the rear entry is the only remnant of the earthen floor tradition. The house has been taken over by raised floors of tatami or of boards, on which street shoes are not worn. In most traditional farmhouses and townhouses, areas which used to have dirt floors have been covered over with planks. The use of the earthen floor for workspace or traffic space has also disappeared. In itself the demise of this type of floor is acceptable, but if in this process of elimination the earthen floor comes to be regarded as something dark and cold and mean, then it is necessary to present an explanation of its former status in Japan.

These days it is fashionable in the West to wear slippers in the home. I don't know whether this has anything to do with the increase in the number of Westerners who have lived in Japan, but at any rate it is quite convenient to step into a pair of slippers to walk around indoors. It is true that slippers and even the word for them were imported into Japan from the West, but in the West, where they are often called "bedroom slippers," their use is basically limited to the bedroom and the adjacent bathroom. In the West, to wear slippers into the living room or dining room is considered bad manners. Only children or the elderly or sick normally wear slippers outside the bedroom area. Shoes are worn in the living room or dining room.

In the West, those people who actually walk around in their homes in slippers do not change their slippers for various rooms as Japanese do. In Japan, different types of slippers are laid out for use when going from the interior rooms into the kitchen, a corridor, a bathroom or onto a veranda or balcony. One then changes from one pair of slippers to another. In the West slippers are viewed almost as personal clothing, but in Japan slippers are a sort of public vehicle. As a Japanese moves about the house, he will often be required by custom to change slippers. For example, when a Japanese enters the toilet, he takes off the hallway slippers and puts on the toilet slippers. This custom came about because the Japanese began long ago to wear *tabi* (Japanese socks with a separate stall for the big toe), and considered such footwear as a type of outerwear. Whether one wears or does not wear slippers over *tabi* is not particularly important. Slippers can be worn over *tabi* in a supplementary fashion. If it is difficult to imagine slippers as "vehicles," then let us say that slippers are a type of "covering," similar to *geta* (wooden clogs) or *zori* (traditional sandals worn with kimono). Inside the residential area, the Japanese have special clogs to wear in the garden, and these, too, are completely public.

It is a serious offense to wear footwear in other than the prescribed places. In Japan, wearing house slippers into the garden, or wearing toilet slippers in the hallway, is not merely impolite but taboo. In each space, the Japanese wear the footwear designated for that space. To remind one of this, there is a slight difference in floor levels between different types of spaces: for example between the vestibule and the corridor, the corridor and the sitting room, the sitting room and the veranda, the sitting room and the toilet or bathroom. As one steps from one type of floor to another, the difference in height in the floor makes it clear that there is a difference in function, and one should wear the appropriate footwear according to that function.

This sort of traditional spatial arrangement is very old. In ancient Japanese society with its strict social class order, the difference in the floor level of a space would by itself define the relative status of the people who used it. For example, the word in Japanese for a high official of the imperial court, *tenjo-bito*, is a contraction of an older expression meaning "above the floor of the imperial palace." The titles of the various courtiers indicated the sorts of space in which they would attend to their duties: *jodan-no-ma* ("room" for honored guests; see pages 68–69), *tatami-no-ma* ("tatami room"), *itajiki* (wooden floor). Among women, too, those who appeared in the sitting rooms and those who carried the trays in the corridors were of different status.

Opposite the *tenjo-bito* ("on-the-palace-floor people") were the *jige-bito* ("down-to-earth people"). These were the people around the palace, the "humble" servants and employees, who had no official rank. Their lives were restricted to the domain of the earthen floor, and they were not permitted to rise above it. The words of an Edo-period (1603–1867) *senryu* poem describe the lives of lower-class people, whether they lived in mansions or in hovels:

> A lower woman's tears
> Fall to an earthen floor

In the samurai residences and in merchants' homes, too, the "down-to-earthers" held the servant jobs and busied themselves upon earthen floors. It was those spaces which soaked up their sweat and tears.

Similar conditions were not unknown in western society. For example, in a Parisian building of the 18th century, the status of the inhabitants was clearly demarcated by the floor levels. Typically the first (ground) floor would be shops, the second the residences of wealthy people, the third the residences of middle-class salaried officials, the fourth for lower-class salaried officials, and poor laborers lived in the attic. Prescribing status through the use of slightly different floor levels is a major distinguishing characteristic of Japanese interiors.

The common people, who might be disdainfully or humiliatingly called *jige-bito*, were long condemned to carry out their lives on earthen floors. In the Edo period (1603–1867) most farmhouses had earthen floors. Records from the Tohoku region show that various feudal clans placed restrictions upon the residences of farmers, such as a prohibition in 1789 on wooden floors imposed by the Yonezawa clan in Yamagata Prefecture, or a limit in 1805 of one wooden-floored room set by the Shinjo clan in Yamagata Prefecture. Historically, this contrast between

Two sunken hearths in a traditional farmhouse.

94

"on-the-floor people" and "down-to-earth people" can be traced back to the contrast between "heavenly gods" and "earthly gods." According to the myths in the ancient chronicles, the descendants of heaven (linked with the imperial lineage) called the earthly gods of Yamato who resisted them derisive names such as "cave dwellers" or "dirt spiders." Even after subjugating the earthly gods of Yamato they did not ameliorate the terms. The descendants of heaven, blessed by divine destiny, thoroughly and completely separated themselves from the earthly gods who were stuck fast to the surface of the earth. But was "heaven" really such an exalted place? Was "the earth" really so ignoble? Let us look back to see what really were the overall conditions of life on earthen floors in Japan.

For thousands of years the original inhabitants of Japan spent their lives on earthen floors. But, as is indicated by a line from a song by Yamanoue no Okura (660–733?) dealing with the issue of poverty, it was not dirt pure and simple:

> In bent and leaning huts
> Unfurling straw straight onto the earth.

Of course there was no stone or lime or concrete on the floors as there was in old Europe. Instead the Japanese mixed straw or rice husks with clay and allowed it to harden, creating an earthen floor which was somewhat elastic and thermally insulating. These are decidedly important properties for a floor. In that respect the earthen floor was not such a bad thing. Further, people sat on mats on the earthen floors, the men cross-legged and the women with one knee drawn up. Every day they would sit more or less directly on the floor. This lifestyle is quite different from that of people in Europe or in China, where chairs and beds were used so that the buttocks were not normally in direct contact with the floor. To cope with the cold, the Japanese cut hearths into the floors and built fires which warmed the floor and the room at the same time. Describing life in a mountain village in the Hokuriku region in 1835, anthropologist-literarist Suzuki Bokushi (1770–1842) reported:

> On winter nights they kindle a large fire in the hearth and sleep at its edge. In very cold weather they bring in straw and make it into pouches for sleeping. The wife makes a large pouch in which she sleeps together with her husband. (*Record of the Far North Snows*)

Even today in some districts there are still "sunken spaces" (*ochima* or *ochiza*), which were a feature of farmhouses in the old days. These spaces had walls around them, rice husks or bran on the floor, and a

Cooking pots set in an ordinary traditional stove, or cooking hearth, which was stoked with wood from below.

hearth was cut into the middle of the floor. In winter the entire family slept there together.

When you think about it, the "down-to-earth" people may have been more comfortable than members of the nobility who had descended from the heavens. Wooden-floored buildings raised above the ground were fine in summer, but they must have been terrible in winter, with chilly winds whistling through the cracks in the floors and doors. And since the nobility were separated from the mundane things of life, they had no hearths with which to keep warm. They only had braziers, designed for hand-warming. Bound up in status and falsehoods, surrounded by paintings of paradise on the ceiling and sliding doors, they sat in freezing reality, shivering and pulling down the sleeves of their coverlets. They may have suffered even more when the summer heat reached its peak, and unable to remove their crowns or ornamental clothing, they bathed in their own sweat. For the status-conscious nobles and samurai it wasn't proper to strip down in the heat of summer the way the common people could. We can thus understand the dictum "Build your house for summer" as being aimed at the ruling classes who were stuck in their lives of bondage and fiction.

It was because of the uncomfortable living conditions of the *shinden*-style house that movable *okitatami* (tatami mats) were installed. These were eventually changed to the type of tatami known today which covers the entire floor of the room. In a manner of speaking, the concept of "unfurling straw straight onto the earth," with its benefits of pliability and insulation, was adopted in whole and reconstituted on top of the wooden floor.

In the Asuka (593–710) and Nara (710–94) periods, the resuscitation of the continental lifestyle which they had yearned for was sweepingly carried out. The nobles and bureaucrats had been compelled to convert from the traditional kneeling bow of Japan to the T'ang-style standing bow, and from a floor-based to a chair-based lifestyle, and this too suddenly crumbled apart.

This is how in the Heian period (794–1185) the custom of sitting on the floor became securely established as the residential lifestyle of Japan. However, for the ruling classes sitting on the floor meant wooden floors with tatami spread over them, while for the common people it meant sitting on earthen floors. Thus was born the class distinction between "on-the-floor people" and "down-to-earth people."

Recently a friend of mine built a large house of steel-reinforced concrete. Since the floors and stairs are also made of concrete, his wife complains that although they have carpeted the whole house, her ears ring, her legs feel wobbly and she is easily tired out if she spends the day on her feet working at home. It is important that the entire floor structure has some resilience, for even covering it over with a few centimeters of carpeting, no matter how soft, will not have much effect on the vibrations which reach the head. Instead, it is good for the body to have a rigid surface over a floor which has structural resilience throughout. This is true both for tatami and for beds. High-quality tatami and high-quality mattresses are generally rather rigid. When it comes to wearing slippers in the house, it is best to wear slippers with thick soles like those of shoes, because the sole itself is resilient and will absorb the shocks involved in walking. This is probably one reason why Westerners wear shoes in the house. Here again, life is not so simple that we can simply despise the humble earthen floor and bring in the carpets.

Ceilings

When the Japanese begin thinking about the home of their dreams and sit down with graph paper to try their hand at residential design, they normally come up with a floor plan. For most Japanese, the ability to sketch out a floor plan seems to comes naturally somehow.

This is due at least in part to the fact that the main parts of the Japanese house are composed of standardized tatami mats, and people in general have acquired the ability to conceive the size of a room according to the number of tatami. After all, only the Japanese have developed floor area specifications which are based on tatami. But when it comes to sensing measurements in three dimensions, a number of problems arise. Certainly three-dimensional measurements are more difficult to express in a drawing than two-dimensional areas, and perhaps it is also difficult to acquire such a sensibility. However, if after a building has been completed it seems different from the way it looked in the drawings, if it feels smaller, or if it isn't very comfortable, there is a better than even chance that the problem lies in the ceiling height, that is, in the three-dimensional size. When Japanese people think of designing their own houses, it is very unusual for them to give any consideration to ceiling height. When it comes to residential planning, the difference between a layperson and a professional architect, aside from the amount of knowledge, boils down to a sensitivity to three-dimensional measurements. To put it briefly, if the ceiling height is not set in designing a two-story house, then the height per story is not set. If the height per story is not set, then the height of the staircase is not set. If the height of the staircase is not set, then its position, and therefore the floor plan of the house, cannot, strictly speaking, be determined. This is why the skilled professional will first decide the ceiling height and the height per story, then estimate the general position and shape of the staircase, and only then tackle the floor plan.

Some people might believe that all ceiling heights are about the same anyway. Therefore we ought to consider an example that will help us understand the problem. Let us consider the construction of the traditional Japanese tearoom, which was developed originally as a place of pleasure for the rich. In most countries the homes and pastimes of the rich tend toward the stately and luxurious, but in Japan the rich took delight in recreating the humble country dwelling, that is the "world of the poor." It is immediately clear upon stepping inside a traditional detached thatch-roofed tearoom that it is an awfully small and cramped space. The walls are earthen and there are no decorations to be seen except in the alcove. The *shitaji-mado*, a window which looks basically as if it were made as an imitation of a hole ripped into the wall, is often used. The main purpose of this type of window is to allow guests to appreciate moonlight pouring through a hole torn into the wall of a rural cottage. It seems as if the rich were amusing themselves by spending the day pretending they were impoverished.

Within this small building, which is based on the principle of honest poverty and simplicity, there is one part of the interior space which is particularly, and complexly, full of variety. It is the ceiling. The ceiling of the tearoom is normally divided into three sections: *shin* (formal style), *gyo* (cursive style) and *so* (flowing style). The guest squeezes through the very low entrance door and steps up onto the tatami mat entryway. Above this entrance mat there is usually a *kakekomi* ceiling which slopes gently upward from the low edge of the eaves toward the center of the room. The pitch of the roof is slightly different from that of other parts of the building in order to make the space of the tearoom seem slightly higher to the guest who has just entered. This is the *so*, or "flowing ceiling." Above the part of the room which faces onto the alcove, or picture recess, is the *shin*, or main ceiling, which is more or less 2 meters (6.5 feet high). Above the space where the host remains seated at all times during a tea ceremony to prepare and serve the tea is the *gyo* ceiling, a false ceiling which is slightly lower. Separate ceilings are also provided for the service entrance and for the alcove; thus within this tiny room (typically four and a half tatami; about 9 square meters or 97 square feet) there are many different ceiling heights. In addition to height variations, each ceiling has a different form and is made from different materials.

The explanation of why this tiny thatched hermitage has so many different ceilings also needs to be divided into several parts. In short, the ceiling height over each section of the room has been reduced as much as possible in order to achieve an appropriate match between the special

Ceiling of a teahouse divided into three sections: *shin* (formal style; here at the right), *gyo* (cursive style; left) and *so* (flowing style; back). Omote Senke Fushin-an, rebuilt 1913.

feeling and the activity which is to be carried out in that section. Since the teahouse gave rise to the *sukiya* style of construction which is usually incorporated in the Japanese-style home, it is understandable that this basic conception of the ceiling still survives. (The *sukiya* style was developed by aristocrats from the *shoin* style, which was influenced by the teahouse. It emphasized understatement and irregularity—and even rusticity.) In the orthodox Japanese-style home, the design forms and materials as well as the height of the ceiling, are different in every room.

In addition to varying the height of the ceiling to correspond to the activities which are carried out in the room, the Japanese also tend to overfill their rooms with furniture. The result is that the typical Japanese low ceiling, which stands in contrast to the high ceilings preferred in most other countries, makes a room seem even more cluttered and cramped. Once when I was in Germany I was proudly explaining the advantages of the Japanese home. When I was finished, someone asked me how high the ceiling was. When I answered, "Usually about 2.3 meters [7.5 feet]," everyone in the room responded with an "Ahh!" and an amused smile. Of course I knew that ceilings in Europe are usually between 2.7 and 3 meters (9 feet to 10 feet) high, but I think the real reason behind their laughter was that I was presenting the low ceiling as one of the advantages of the Japanese home. What we have here, I believe, is a cultural difference.

The European preference for high ceilings can be at least partially understood from the etymology of the word: the English "ceiling" comes from the French "ciel," which comes from the Latin "caelum," sky. Indeed, the Gothic cathedral in which the ceiling seems to reach to the sky is the basic ideal that a ceiling is intended to meet. In fact, in ancient Japan as well, the preference was for high ceilings. The homes of clan leaders in ancient times, which were related to the shrine architecture of antiquity, didn't have flat ceilings. Later, however, under the influence of Chinese architecture, the flat ceiling appeared in Japan. The *gotenjo* was a ceilinglike element which had been adopted from China. Called a "dust collector" in old Chinese sources, it was used in Japanese temples and sanctuaries for that function and also as an upper anchor for latticework. The Chinese shared the European ideal of the ceilings that reach toward the heavens. Under Chinese influence, the *gotenjo* of Japan were much higher than ceilings of today and were decorated with colored paintings of goddesses, the dragon king or a mountain sunrise. Special care was often taken to make the ceiling complex and interesting, as if showing off the inside of a hat, and this was another factor that contributed to high ceilings.

But the architectural style which initiated the complete turnabout toward today's preference for low ceilings of varying heights was the *sukiya* style, which, as mentioned earlier, grew out of the tearoom. The ultimate source was the thatched cottage upon which tearoom architecture was modeled, or more precisely the dwelling design of the common people.

In common dwellings, the ability to make and maintain a fire was important. Whatever else might be lacking, as long as there was fire and shelter from the weather—a roof—people could somehow survive. From the ancient times of pit dwellings onward, the central element of the common house was fire, which is to say that a stove or hearth was indispensable. Here we encounter the other stream of the history behind the Japanese house, which stands in complete contrast to the series of dwellings used by the ruling classes in which defense and status were the main concerns.

In the old commoners' residences, a latticelike framework of thick pieces of wood, usually called a *hidana*, was typically suspended over the hearth. These were used for drying anything from brushwood and kindling to herbs and fruit and even clothing or straw sandals, as well as for smoking meat or fish. This practice was not limited to the area over the hearth; many homeowners spread a network of bamboo slats across the whole upper section of the room to form a type of ceiling, usually known as an *amada*. The area above the slats came to be used for storage, in which case it was known as an *amadana*.

My own supposition is that the *amada* was the genesis of the low ceiling, which was counter to the "ideal of reaching toward the heavens." My theory is that people for whom "facing heaven" is important would abhor placing things overhead which would abstract the upward view, but this did not faze the ancient Japanese. Among the indigenous Japanese there was no such ideal. The spirits of ancestors were believed to be in the earth or beyond the sea, not in heaven. The orientation of the sacred was horizontal, not vertical. In contrast to the continental ideal, these ideals seem to be befitting an island nation, ideals which could be described as earth-oriented or sea-oriented.

It is clear that people would not be particularly concerned about placing kindling or sacks or tools or whatever overhead. Instead it was simply common sense that indicated that the dryness of the air above the fireplace made it an excellent storage area, and that among the common people a utilization of such space was also highly efficient. That is precisely the ideal of the tearoom. Thinking along those lines, we notice the close resemblance between the materials often used for the ceiling of a

A sunken hearth with a *hidana* (lattice
framework of thick pieces of wood)
above.

Amadana storage area above a slatted
ceiling (*amada*).

Hooded vents on the roof of a farmhouse.

teahouse—such as bamboo slats and various reeds, and those used in the *amada* rack structures of the commoners' homes. The source of the low ceiling may well be entirely different from the generation and progression of the high ceiling.

Furthermore, the racklike ceilings of the commoners' homes did not necessarily take the same form in each room. In townhouses, for example, there is a hooded vent at the roof level. The first-floor ceiling stops short of the hearth or kitchen area, allowing the warm air to rise and exit through the vent. This not only helped rid the interior of smoke from the fire but also facilitated air circulation. Usually the ceilings of the sitting rooms were not racklike structures but rather planks set across the beams. The *amada* racks, or rather the ceilings into which they developed (the floor planks of second-story storage areas), were found only in other rooms. In short, if there was a racklike low ceiling in the various rooms of the common dwelling, there was also a ventilating high ceiling. If there was a proper ceiling, there was also one which supported a second-floor storage area. These sorts of ceiling variations seemed to

Interior and exterior views of a townhouse smoke vent.

allow the expelling of smoke, the preserving of heat, the storing of goods, the receiving of guests or the providing of other practical services. In other words, a ceiling was not good simply because it was too high or too low. It was an important structural element which allowed the room to fulfill a given function. This leads us to the idea that the creation of teahouse architecture, imitating the common residential architecture, may not merely have been a rich man's attempt at "tasting poverty" but something connected to the rediscovery of the indigenous Japanese culture.

From a wider perspective, the height of the ceiling in contemporary residential design may be worth some further consideration. There is a fundamental difference in perspective, due to differing eye levels, between the Japanese, who sit on the floor, and the Chinese and Westerners, who sit on chairs, which naturally means that the ceiling height which provides the optimal sense of security will also differ. This certainly seems to be one reason for the low ceilings in Japanese homes. Moreover, with today's growing trend toward mixing—some would say confusing—Japanese and western styles in the same home, this factor cannot be ignored. If the ceiling of a Japanese-style room is too high, the Japanese somehow find it uncomfortable. On the other hand, the atmosphere of a western room with a typical low Japanese ceiling can become oppressive, as if it were difficult to breathe.

The important thing to remember for a Japanese room is not so much the ceiling but the elevation of the windows. Low-set windows functioning to widen the sense of space are needed, whereas in a western room it is the ceiling height which is the decisive factor. In other words, while a Japanese room becomes bigger along the horizontal axes, a western room expands vertically. For a Japanese room, as the area becomes smaller it is appropriate to lower the ceiling, while for a western room the opposite is true—the smaller the floor area, the higher the ceiling needs to be. These are the types of three-dimensional-design issues that need to be considered in order to avoid creating oppressive spaces.

Nowadays in the West, where it has long been thought that ceilings should be high, there is a trend toward lower ceilings. I wonder if this represents a reversal of the historical trend away from the spiritualistic "ideal of facing heaven" and toward the materialistic respect for temporal life. At any rate, we have known for 600 years, thanks to the sage Yoshida Kenko (1283–1350), that "high ceilings make for cold winters and dim lighting."

Stairways

If you walk down the back streets of central Kyoto you can still find peaceful rows of old-fashioned houses with low-hanging eaves, small second-story windows and latticework doors. Some of them are row houses—two-story homes linked with common walls and a single roof—but for the most part they are the separate, freestanding townhouses. Although they are freestanding, the walls facing each other come right together without so much as a crack between them, in order to make the most of their narrow sites.

If you have a chance to enter one of these townhouses, you will probably find the interior larger and brighter than you expected. The furnishings are very likely to be not only firmly built and of fine quality, but also carefully arranged. Of course, it feels much more homey, much more opulent, than a modern prefab house. Known informally and somewhat derisively as ''eels' bedrooms,'' the townhouses are narrow yet deep from front to back. The farther back you go, the finer the house, the finer the garden; indeed, the more refined the whole house appears to become. This is the Kyoto townhouse or *machiya*: easy to dismiss at first glance as a modest structure, hardly different from a row house, yet as splendid inside as a mansion.

The *machiya* were originally tradesmen's homes out of which the tradesmen worked. The facade is often concealed by a fence or a pine tree. The interior is quite different from the barracklike simplicity of a samurai home. Although the exterior of the townhouse is simple, the interior, just as you would expect of a merchant, is unsparingly extravagant. Here we glimpse the city dweller's spirit of valuing substance over appearance. It is not simply that the interior decor is excellent, but that the long, narrow space is used in a entirely logical manner. To give an example, almost all of the rooms are entered by stepping up from an earthen-floored corridor, which runs straight from the front to the rear of the house, so that there is no need to traverse one room to reach another. The independence and privacy of these rooms are rare in a Japanese residence.

This sort of urban residence exhibits a spatial pattern and rationality perfect for a home constructed in a neighborhood jam-packed with other buildings. Yet there is one part of the townhouse space which has not been so well managed, and that is the stairway. The townhouse stairway may not look so bad at first, for it has quite an interesting design, being hidden in a closet (and therefore called a "box stair") with the lower end camouflaged to look like a cabinet. But the staircase has two significant problems. One is placement within the overall house design.

In a townhouse, the stairway is in the kitchen, also called the center room because this wooden-floored room is exactly in the center of the house. The stairway is usually located on the wall opposite the earth-floored corridor. Therefore it is necessary to cross the kitchen, which is usually where meals are taken, to reach the second floor. Since merchandise is often stored on the second floor, clerks frequently have to go upstairs, even right in the middle of a meal. Consequently, the opening for the lower stairway is located near both the shop (the front room) and the sitting room (the back room). The stairway also doubles back for easy access from the front. Now the tradesmen's townhouses have become standardized in most areas down to the last detail, so that every house maintains the same arrangements and spatial rhythms. But there are still an infinite variety of stairways. Each household has drawn on its own resources of wisdom, yet the design of these staircases never seems to improve. The fact is that in the townhouse, the stairway is an embarrassing nuisance that no one has ever really figured out how to use effectively.

Secondly, when we try to climb up that nuisance of a staircase, it seems that we do so at great risk. On this rattling and shaking "stairway in a box" one is never quite sure of his footing, and the sensation of total darkness inside the stair closet can be quite unnerving. Furthermore, the steps are quite steep, and usually there is neither a handrail nor a lamp. As a child growing up in a townhouse in Hikone in Shiga Prefecture, climbing the stairs meant steadying myself on the stairs ahead with one hand and tightly gripping a candle with the other, staring upward, listening to my grandmother admonishing me loudly about something or other, and all in all feeling as if I were getting ready to die.

When you think about it, this sort of thing is not limited to the townhouse. As a general rule, the stairways of Japanese houses are

Earthen floor corridor (bottom right) allows access to a number of rooms in the *machiya* townhouse.

Box stair in a *machiya* townhouse.

Precarious ladderlike stairway
typically found in townhouses.

clumsy and dangerous. Even in the old multistoried castle structures,
the upward turns of the stairways to the tower were perilous.

In comparison, the stairways in western houses are usually well constructed. The cinema cliché of a broad stairway leading up from the
front hall of the house is quite familiar to the Japanese, even if much of
the audience may feel as if they are looking at an impossibly huge
fairyland stairway. Although the stairway of the average western home
may not be quite so spectacular, in most cases it is stoutly constructed.
What is more, it is often centrally located within the house, and can
serve as an important part of the living space. Of course films and plays
tend to be more dramatic than everyday life, but still it is noteworthy
that western filmmakers often use stairways as settings for key scenes in
their films. The camera may follow someone upward, step by step, as a
means of building tension, or the stairway may be the stage for the tear-
ful farewell of lovers who are torn apart by circumstance, or a fight in
which someone falls to his death. As a general rule, the appearance of a
stairway on the screen foreshadows a climactic scene of some sort. What
is more, I have heard from various acquaintances that when emotions
flare up in everyday life, it is not at all unusual for the persons involved
to use the stairway as a corridor of approach, escape or at least communication during their spat.

In Japan, the stairway as a stage for dramatic action is not unknown. A well-known example is the classic Kabuki play *The Love Suicides at Sonezaki*, in which a courtesan, pursuing her lover, gropes her way up a stairway in the black of night. In old Japan, where only large inns and pleasure houses had what could be called proper stairways, a stage heroine would not be dramatically thrown down them by someone else, but rather, she would lose her own footing while tiptoeing down, thereby waking up her husband. Even in tragic plays, such moments are played slightly comically. This is indicative of the stairway's mightiest achievement in traditional Japanese housing. The Japanese stairway is not a sociable place where people hold dialogues, but is rather a place for expressing the deeply hidden nuances of the individual psyche.

This difference in the significance of the stairway between Japan and the West can be traced back to the very origin of the staircase. The anthropologist Tadao Umesao (1920–   ) has pointed out that there are two possible origins for the Japanese staircase. According to one theory, the staircase was a sort of ladder or bridge. In its earliest form it was made by chopping serrations as footholds into a log with a hatchet, producing what might be termed a three-dimensional bridge; indeed, the old Japanese word for this type of stairway, *kizahashi*, includes *hashi*, the word for "bridge." Archaeological relics at Toro, Shizuoka Prefecture, suggest that just such devices were exclusively used to climb in and out of ancient raised-floor dwellings, and one interpretation of the original form of the Izumo Taisha Shrine in Shimane Prefecture included a stairway several times as high as the main building itself. In the course of time this became the Japanese "ladder," then boards were added along both sides to produce "ladder stairs." Finally backboards were attached to produce the "box stairs" which serve as the stairways of most traditional wooden houses to this day. According to this ladder theory, from the beginning the Japanese stairway has simply been a means or a route of ascent and descent. The way in which this type of stairs was traversed in ancient times was not the contemporary system of placing the feet alternately on the notches. Instead people turned their bodies slightly sideways and placed both feet on each step. Shinto priests still do this when they are returning from audiences with the imperial court. If people had not moved up and down the staircase in this manner, they not only would have had difficulty keeping their balance when going up and down the narrow, steep ladder stairway, but the length of the ancient kimono hems would also have hampered the person climbing or descending such a stairway.

Primitive ladder (*kizahashi*) used for raised storehouses.

The other source of the Japanese staircase was the platform style which can be seen in temples of both eastern and western civilizations. In the Aztec temples of Mexico, for example, steps were cut into a man-made platform of earth and stones, which was shaped like the bottom portion of a pyramid. Often a sanctuary, a temple or a shrine was erected on top. The stone platform of Horyuji Temple in Nara Prefecture is a well-known Japanese example. This is an ancient style, believed to have originated more than 5,000 years ago in Mesopotamia, where a series of artificial hills were built up on a broad plain, and a temple was erected on each one. Excavation has revealed that they were not made simply of earth and stone but were actually built on the accumulated remains of reed huts, brick dwellings and the like. Apparently at each site a village was constructed and destroyed, rebuilt and again destroyed many times and gradually accumulated into a hill. There we have the accumulation of history before our very eyes, and this seems to be part of the reason why the ground was sanctified. The artificial hills may well have influenced later landmarks like the Ziggurat hill temples of Babylonia and the pyramids of Egypt, as the direct ancestors of the manmade stairway platform. The style culminated in the beautiful temples of ancient Greece and the dignified palace buildings of China built on mounds of clay or earth.

The stairway in such a platform context was more than a simple route of ascent and descent; it had significance as a sort of sacred ground. Accordingly, the halls which were typically erected on top of these platforms were designed to strongly attract the human eye. Thus the platform-style staircase took on a social significance as a link between the world of the high (the sacred) and the world of the low (the secular). This characteristic as a space connecting different levels of society was passed on to Europe as well as to the East.

In European architecture, the ground floor is usually a public space. In the home, it is the site of the larger, common-use rooms for eating and gathering. The master bedroom is typically located one floor up. The staircase linking the main public space and the main private space is highly visible, not very steep, wide enough for two people to pass and, means permitting, nicely finished with perhaps an attractive balustrade, carpeting or paintings hanging along the walls. If there is another staircase linking, say, the second and third stories of the house, it is likely to be a simpler affair. This is due to the tendency for social status to decline as the level of the dwelling space rises, with children, boarders and servants likely to live in ascending order above the parents. The levels which the staircase serves to connect have social as well as physical dimensions.

In Japan, on the other hand, it seems that careful design consideration is given to concealing the location of the stairs. The ideal is the "hidden staircase." Since the ladder-stairway of ancient Japanese homes could not be hidden no matter what was done, it was only in later years that Japan moved away from the European-style consciousness of social stratification based upon the floor level.

In any case, it is a fact that in the contemporary Japanese house the stairway still tends to be treated shabbily, locked away from the light of day. When they design the second floor of a home, people want to economize on space as much as possible. Sometimes they forget that a stairway is a three-dimensional space: staircases which seem designed for headless people may be encountered in restaurants and bars as well as in private homes. Moreover while it is easy enough to spot the elevator in a hotel, department store or apartment building, finding the stairs is often a mysterious process. The ideal of the "hidden stairway'' may be epitomized in the traditional townhouse, but it is certainly still flourishing in today's modern architecture.

In the home, the salient characteristic of the stairway may well be danger. Most Japanese children have had the experience of falling down the stairs; children are resilient, but should an elderly person happen to fall, he or she may never fully recover. In case of disaster in a larger building, the ''missing'' stairway invites greater tragedy.

In Europe the great stone steps of cathedrals and the like are no longer functioning to indicate differences in social or spiritual levels, but instead they are becoming three-dimensional public spaces where people from all walks of life mingle and relax. Likewise, as Japanese architecture shifts its emphasis from flatness toward three-dimensionality, it is high time to renovate the image of the residential stairway, to bring it out of its dark and dangerous hiding place onto center stage as an enjoyable part of a multi-storied dwelling.

Upper Stories

The house where I spent my childhood was a shop in Hikone in Shiga Prefecture. Even at that time it had been standing for more than a century. The second story, which my grandmother referred to as the *tsushi*, was a low, dark space with no ceiling. "*Tsushi*" is an old-fashioned term meaning "high place." At any rate, it does not refer to an upstairs space with a ceiling used for normal living purposes. During the Edo period (1603–1867) various prohibitions against luxury and ostentation were promulgated as part of the enforcement of the rigid social order. The shoguns and lords were opposed to commoners having a second floor where fancy possessions could be kept, or where people could look down upon passing samurai. Consequently, the residences of the common Japanese did not have proper second floors until the time of the Meiji Restoration (1868) when the shogunate fell.

The homes of the privileged samurai and ruling classes did not have second stories either. Even in the handsome castle towers which stood three or five stories high, the stairways were too steep and tortuous for everyday use. It is my view that the traditional Japanese kimono was simply not suited to life in multistoried structures because one always had to take great pains to avoid stepping on the hem. It just wouldn't do to hold up the hem when going up or down the stairs. It was easier for the samurai to move up and down stairs because they usually wore more convenient skirtlike *hakama*, except when they donned their formal palace clothing, which trailed slightly on the floor.

Another problem with the stairways in the old castle towers was that, although they were affixed above and below with metal fittings, the fittings were not securely bolted into place. This allowed the stairs to be dismantled and dropped in an emergency. The tower space was not intended to serve the castle residents as a living space, but rather as an uncomfortable haven to which they could escape in a crisis. The stairs between levels were in fact provisional structures which could be drawn up to thwart the enemy from ascending to the higher level. In short, a castle tower was a fortress. The Japanese warriors carried out their daily duties in a separate one-story building below the fortifications.

It was the same with the temples. The tops of Chinese temple buildings are noted for having observation towers with fine views. But in Japan such halls and pagodas are only to be looked up at. The example that symbolizes this best is the Golden Hall of Horyuji Temple in Nara Prefecture, which also happens to be the oldest building in Japan. This building appears to be a two-story structure, but there are no floorboards for a second story. It is purely an illusion to be viewed from outside. This concept extends to all the various temple pagodas of Japan as well. They are primarily monuments and works of visual art. There is no question of enjoying the view from the top story. The five-story pagoda at Kofukuji Temple in Nara Prefecture has a relatively substantial staircase, but there is no space for people other than in the stairwell itself. The Eastern Pagoda of Yakushiji Temple in Nara Prefecture doesn't have stairs running up it. When necessary, arrangements would be made for passage between the roof and the third story. Such truncated stairways may have been designed partly as a means to discourage vagrants from camping in the buildings.

Not only in residences, then, but in various types of Japanese buildings, with the exception of two or three examples which will be cited below, there were no habitable upper stories. From the earliest times right up to the 19th century, Japanese architecture seems to have been almost entirely a one-story affair.

Outside of Japan we find the world's oldest known laws, the Babylonian Code of Hammurabi, specified that if someone suffered a broken limb because the second story of a structure collapsed or the floor gave way, then the carpenter who built it would be similarly injured. If the accident was serious enough to kill someone, then the carpenter was to be executed. Thus we know that second stories were already in existence nearly 4,000 years ago—and that they could be dangerous. In the Roman Empire there were frequent official prohibitions of shoddy construction practices for tall buildings, which tells us that some progress had been made, but still leaves us with the overall feeling that in antiquity, when construction technology was not very advanced, a multistory design was rather dangerous. Such designs would have been especially dangerous in Japan, where land subsidence and earthquakes are frequent phenomena, and this is probably the key reason why the second story was never developed.

The Golden Pavilion.

Urbanization is the main reason why people began erecting high buildings. Babylon and Rome were both cities with very large populations which necessitated vertical expansion. But it seems that there was another reason as well, one which becomes evident if we look at the exceptional cases in which two-story buildings did appear in Japan, despite the traditional commitment to architecture on one plane.

The first of the very few pre-Meiji (pre–1868) cases of a residential second story was the pavilion-style aristocratic residences during the Muromachi period (1333–1573). The buildings which eventually became the Kinkakuji (the Golden Pavilion) and Ginkakuji (the Silver Pavilion) are the finest examples. If we consider these buildings residential, we should point out that, strictly speaking, they were villas

Gifu Castle with its third-floor tearoom and fourth-floor lookout.

equipped with watchtowers for viewing gardens which were never intended for everyday living. In the late 16th century, the strongholds constructed by Oda Nobunaga (1534–82) and Toyotomi Hideyoshi (1536–98) were ornate, extravagant multistory palaces. In Gifu Castle, the first of these, the second floor was the husband's retiring room, the third floor a tearoom and the fourth a lookout. These teahouses were designed as great teahouse palaces in the relatively informal "*daimyo* tea" style of the time. Next came the brothels for the common people and the inns which developed during the Edo period. In these structures the guests went upstairs, but the assignation rooms or guest rooms on the second floor were regarded as special spaces. An interesting aspect of the world of pleasure of that time was that on the second floor it was per-

Ukiyo-e drawing depicting a house of pleasure. Note the second-floor meeting area where class differences could be temporarily transcended.

missible to violate the strict class order. In order to negotiate the stairs more easily the maidservants of the inns would tuck up their kimonos and expose their red undergarments as they moved about with the trays of food and drink. The final example is, again, the tradesmen's homes of the Edo period. The upper part of a typical large townhouse at that time was not used so much as a second-story living area but for storage and perhaps also as a sleeping area for servants. Properly speaking, the upper floor should be called an attic. But there were some exceptions: sometimes in the rearmost storehouse of a *machiya* townhouse, the ground floor or the second floor would be made into sitting rooms. These were typically used as places to display refined collections of paintings and curios, for it was at this point in history that the tradesmen became wealthy enough to cultivate aesthetic pursuits. Ihara Saikaku's (1642–93) *Nippon eitai gura* ("Japanese Storehouses Through the Ages"; 1688) discloses that some of the *nouveau riche* even had three-story storehouses.

This survey of the few cases of upstairs rooms in old Japan shows that, whether villa or palace, brothel or inn or salon, the upper story(ies) was not used for normal everyday living but for special entertainment. They were festive, not ordinary, spaces. Japanese at that time thought that the world, which was separated from the earth's surface and for which they removed their shoes, was a very pleasurable one.

This was because pleasure was considered to be a feeling associated with illusion. Furthermore, the urge for escape from the earth where one groveled and toiled daily was also linked to spiritual aspirations.

Yet the use of the second story as a pleasure space seems not to have come about merely as a spiritual impulse. Particular physical reasons can also be cited. In the first place, there was the view from the upper stories which aroused the spirit of illusion. Even today, the top floor of a hotel commands a higher price. Also, the ventilation was better, and this was an important point in humid Japan. When it came to storing a collection of painted scrolls and wooden carvings, it was only common sense that they be placed where damage from humidity and insects was least likely—on the second floor of the storehouse. The third factor is that the second story offered favorable exposure to the sun.

It was not just that the second floor was an environment well suited to recreation, but also that a specific need in Japanese life could be fulfilled—the need for a pleasurable space. Every once in a while, the privileged people of the time would get tired of their everyday humdrum lifestyle on the first floor and go upstairs to renew their energy level. Indeed, in the technologically advanced Japan of today, it might be a good idea to give more thought to such second-floor living.

It was not until about 1920 that the general population of Japan began to experience homes with second floors in the form of the *bunka jutaku* (''culture home'') which was aimed at the middle- and upper-level office workers of the modernizing economy. Besides having the functions enumerated above, the second floor offered a certain amount of privacy that was not available before. The two-floor house became very popular in the period before World War II. As the scale of the residence was reduced after the war, the Japanese settled back into their traditional single-plane homes. With the recent rapid increases in the prices of homes and property, the second floor has come back into vogue. In contrast to the comfortable space in the *sukiya* tradition, which was the hallmark of the second floor in the cultural homes of the 1920s, the fully modern two-story-type house tends to be an inelegant, storehouselike structure. Not only that, but with each owner building his house in the middle of a tiny site as he pleases, the poor use of land also contributes to the space problem. The houses are built in such a way that they bump right up against each other to the point where a person has to think twice about opening a window. This sort of mindless three-dimensionalizing of the home falls far short of bringing out the full potential of second-story living.

In the West, residents of freestanding homes try to make maximum use of the space around the building. Many two-story homes are designed to have gardens and entryways on opposite sides of the building. One even runs across such elegant touches as a second-floor bathtub placed so as to offer the bather full enjoyment of the garden scenery. It is growing more and more necessary for the Japanese to give up their insistence on traditional "single-level homes" and to devote their energies to considering ways in which interior space can be used more efficiently, conceiving and devising second-floor designs which are suitable for them.

A harmonious mixture of *sukiya*-style and pagoda-style roofs. Choshukaku.

Rooftops

I constantly find myself thinking how beautiful the Japanese city would be if modern buildings did not have flat roofs.

The Japanese city underwent a complete change of appearance in the decades following World War II. I saw an American newsreel in Japan just after the end of the war which I will never forget. It showed a Japanese city after an air raid, reduced to scorched earth from which smoke and flames were rising. A few incendiary bombs were sufficient to transform our wood-and-paper towns into burned-out wildernesses in virtually no time at all. The only recognizable features were crumbling storehouses, slanting electric poles and mutilated signboards. Otherwise there was nothing but heaps of rubble. The words which were superimposed on the screen were forever burned into my eyes: "Last gasp of the unscientific."

What a pitiful condemnation of the cities of a defeated nation! Such was the world's view of Japan at the time. When you think about it, on top of losing the war, this sort of thing came not only as a shock but also as an insult to Japanese culture.

A quarter of a century later, Japanese cities were lined with multistory structures. The number of fires had decreased, and in particular, Japan's famous great urban fires had become a thing of the past. For Japanese cities had been transformed into steel and concrete. But nowadays foreigners frequently offer the criticism that Japanese cities are among the world's ugliest. Indeed, I myself found, upon returning from travels to foreign cities, especially in Europe, that Japanese cities seem hideous. From today's vantage point, it seems that whatever was lacking in terms of fire-prevention standards, the old-fashioned wood-and-paper cities did have their special flavor and beauty. The large number of young Japanese tourists visiting the surviving castle

Tile roofs, a common scene before World War II.

towns and post towns shows that I am not alone in my opinion.

But there is no going back. We have to accept the present circumstances as the foundation for any speculation about the future. Looking at the Japanese city from that perspective, I find that the biggest single factor behind the ugliness is the rooftop space of the multistory office blocks and apartment buildings.

Nowadays the lack of urban beauty is widely discussed, even in the newspapers. The subject that receives the most attention is the *biru*, or the modern building, which stands five to ten stories high. The question usually boils down either to harmonizing such modern buildings with traditional Japanese architecture, or to harmonizing them with other high-rise structures. These five-to-ten-story buildings are often at the heart of the controversy over urban beauty, for they have become the major component of Japan's city centers. Naturally it is impossible to have a meaningful discussion without taking them into account.

The rooftops of these mid-rise buildings are especially ugly. Recently the shapes and materials of the exterior walls have become quite attractive, but if you look at the rooftops, they are truly hideous. On the tops of those buildings are penthouses covered with mortar or some similarly colorless finish, water storage tanks that have faded to gray and grotesquely shaped cooling towers (both of which are supported by rusty iron frames or pipes), a forest of television antennae sprouting like mold and sometimes prefab huts and small poles full of drying laundry. Rising vertically, as if to sneer at the painstaking design of the building on which it stands, may be a giant advertising tower or a garish neon sign, which if viewed from the rear present a jungle of steel skeletons that overwhelms the building below it. The rooftop looks like a combination of a rubbish heap and the back side of a stage set.

The situation in a European city is usually very different. To put it simply, a four- or five-story building in Europe usually has a roof. I mean a proper sloping roof, such that the rooftop is not a place upon which things can be easily mounted or placed. Of course, this has much to do with the fact that many European buildings are quite old, but new buildings also show evidence of similar consideration. For example, many publicly subsidized apartment complexes with lines which are quite modern have pergola-style roofs. Well then, what about the New World? In American city centers there tend to be many high-rise buildings, and there are flat rooftops of various heights which are sometimes utilized as parking garages or heliports, which are usually almost invisible from below. Very tall buildings often have restaurants or other public spaces on the top floors, and a flat roof above them, where no one other than the building staff is allowed. These rooftop spaces are constructively utilized for various purposes, and are not treated as catchall spaces as in Japan. Thus we see that the unattractive spaces atop Japanese mid-rise buildings are in fact an unwelcome specialty of Japan. The Japanese city has not become "scientific," but has instead lost its beauty. What must be considered now is the question of what the city and its architecture should be.

I was once invited to a party celebrating the completion of a magnificent new house measuring some 200 square *tsubo* (about 660 square meters, or 7,000 square feet). It was a western-style structure with a flat roof, and that is where the party was held. The view was splendid. At one corner of the rooftop there was a tearoom, and this space was evidently the host's pride and joy. Although the house had extravagant

A street scene in Tsumago, an Edo-period post town.

marble floors, the rooftop was covered with the usual Japanese tar paper. Of course the rooftop also had an equipment room with a clamoring air conditioner and bare steel pipes running here and there. A plate of the finest caviar was put out on a table which rocked back and forth on the uneven surface of the tar paper floor—a very strange, yet definitely Japanese, scene.

Although no one has made a precise inspection, Japan probably has a larger area of flat rooftops than any other country in the world. I would guess that the flat rooftops of a single Japanese prefecture would be equal in area to those of an entire European country. This should mean that Japan is a nation with a "rooftop culture." But aside from the children's playgrounds on department store roofs, or the occasional garden on top of some buildings, the Japanese have not had much success in using this space. In the early postwar years there were various schemes for utilizing apartment building rooftops for hanging laundry out to dry or as children's play areas, but very few of these plans materialized. Instead, most of the roofs were put under lock and key in order to prevent burglars from getting onto the top-floor balconies and breaking in. The rooftops were entirely taken over by television antennas, with no signs of human life. Wouldn't it have been preferable to have built sloping roofs, which would have been more attractive and more practical in combating the rain and humidity?

In the Mediterranean where there is little rainfall, evenings were often spent on the rooftops to avoid the heat of the ground and to catch cool breezes. Taking the evening air on the roof became an indispensable part of the lifestyle. But in Japan there is no need to avoid hot desert sands. Instead, in midsummer the radiant heat rising from the concrete-covered earth to the rooftops is enough to soften asphalt.

Flat rooftops probably became popular when western-style buildings spread through Japan because people wanted more space. There is a vague idea that if there is a rooftop, then perhaps it can be put to good use, but in reality it is not so simple to turn the rooftop into a usable space. Aside from the problems of rain, wind and direct sunlight, many people feel acrophobia to some degree. Moreover, in Japan many suicide attempts are made from rooftops and the association may be strong enough to tempt those in a more melancholy mood to jump to their deaths.

As flat rooftops proliferated in Japan, they eventually came to be used mainly for storage and for equipment of one sort or another. But when you think about it, if storage is the goal it would be better to erect a gable roof with an attic space in which all sorts of items could be put and preserved. If advertising is required, then it would be better to integrate the advertising into the architecture, providing the building itself with a superior design which projects an identity and an image. For those who insist upon conventional rooftop advertising signs or towers, they should incorporate the rooftop advertising sign or tower into the overall design of the building.

If the roof is intended for use as a living space, then the rooftop design deserves more serious consideration. For example, in place of railings the rooftop ought to be surrounded with walls which are at least two meters high and finished to some degree; within these wall there should be pergola or trellis structures to provide shelter from rain and sunlight. This would provide full safety and protection against the elements.

I think it is best to abandon the idea of the rooftop as a place for enjoying the scenery. A rooftop which is not prudently managed can, according to one's frame of mind, become an invitation to disaster. For those who really want the scenic view, it can be easily provided by putting glazed windows in the surrounding wall. On apartment buildings, this sort of design would yield a safe play area for children. With walls to screen out the wind, senior citizens could sit in the sun even in winter. In other words, the rooftop can be designed as a sort of room without a roof. The important thing, as with any room, is not to worry excessively about the cost. Without a little added investment, the roof cannot serve for anything other than exposed storage.

Japan should pioneer the development of such rooftop-living space. Because the flat roof has not proliferated to such an extent in any other nation, an available model does not exist.

Clothes-Drying Area

After an architect-designed Japanese house has been built, it has to be photographed before the occupants move in. This is because as soon as they move in, a clothes-drying area is set up and laundry is hung out to dry, spoiling the effect of the exterior design and even turning it into a bit of a joke. It is quite rare to come across a photograph of any type of modern house in an architectural magazine which shows laundry hanging out to dry. In fact one does not often come across a photograph which actually shows a clothes-drying area.

This problem became a topic of discussion just after the war when the steel-reinforced concrete apartment building appeared in Japan. The balconies on the south sides of the brand-new modern apartment buildings were bedecked with diapers and underwear. The builders had provided laundry-hanging space on the rooftops, and they wanted the drying to be done up there. But the housewives simply wouldn't use those facilities, not only because it was troublesome to climb up to the roof, but also because it was difficult to take in the laundry in the event of a sudden rain. As for the critics, some wrote that covering the balconies with laundry marred the beauty of the housing complexes, while others felt that this sort of dynamic, ''lived-in'' appearance was beautiful, or at least natural.

The purists did seem to have a case. For example, in the *machiya* townhouses of Kyoto, from the old days until now, laundry has never been seen in front of the homes. This is not because of some law or regulation. It was simply the custom of the townspeople to dry their laundry in the rear garden, along the back side of the second story, or on a platform set on the roof. Even today one hears stories of students who take rooms in a *machiya* townhouse of Kyoto being admonished by the owners for hanging their trousers in the front windows to dry. This

A typical apartment building with laundry hanging on the balconies and *futon* airing.

is a case of community-minded self-regulation for keeping up the appearance of the neighborhood—something which could serve as a good lesson for the increasingly self-centered Japanese of today.

Here we have a case of "self-imposed controls" which depend upon the efforts of the women, especially the housewives, of the neighborhood. This control depended on the labor of the women which would have escaped the attention of the heads of the households, who were nevertheless likely to be the first to grumble about the unsightliness of the neighborhood.

There is another factor as well. In the old days people had less laundry. The reasons for this did not have much to do with the drying space, but rather that people believed that the more a garment was laundered, the more damage was done to the material. In the days before robust chemical fibers, cotton garments, especially the mixed staple fibers from which socks and other undergarments were made, deteriorated in direct proportion to the number of times they were washed. Furthermore, soap was a very precious commodity. The common people of old Japan would wear their blue-dyed clothes, as long as they were not too obviously soiled, year after year for as long as they could. Nowadays of course that would be considered unclean.

A rooftop drying area.

After the war, when socks and undergarments came to be made of stronger fibers, there was sort of revolution in lifestyle. At the same time, a whole gamut of consumer appliances suddenly became available. Hand in hand with the appearance of the washing machine came a significant increase in the amount of laundry people did compared to the prewar years. These days it seems that the domestic chore that women perform most conscientiously is the laundry. Of course, it is far different from the prewar days when dirt-smeared garments would be gingerly and tiresomely laundered with a basin and washboard, and hands were always chapped by the cold water and deformed from constant repetition of this chore. Now clothes are tossed into a washer with a generous amount of soap, whirled and agitated, taken out and then hoisted high in the sunny, breezy fresh air. There is something quite refreshing about this sight, as if one's own spirit has been washed along with the laundry. A friend of mine coined the witticism "The clothes pole brings one to life." The point is that today, doing the laundry is without a doubt a much more enjoyable household chore than it used to be.

Even so, it does not mean that clothes hung out to dry are enjoyable in an aesthetic sense. People do not find themselves particularly inspired to go for a stroll in a housing-complex garden full of flapping laundry. This still leaves us with two opposing opinions both of which have their merits.

Since Europeans are fussy about their views, drying clothes on the balcony is prohibited in some parts of Europe. Instead they hang them near north-facing windows or inside their rooms. In Northern Europe, where the sun doesn't shine very much, people seldom think of drying clothes in the sun. To their way of thinking, laundry is dried in wind and dry air—or in an electric dryer. Now, most apartment buildings have laundry rooms in the basement, with both washers and dryers, where the whole job can be done at once.

In a similar vein, the Japanese custom of airing the *futon* bedding faces similar criticism. The Japanese will not be easily dissuaded from their deeply rooted conviction that this ''sterilizing and disinfecting'' practice is essential for hygiene, yet a panorama of *futon*s of all colors and patterns hung out on balconies can be an unsettling experience.

I can, however, offer two modest suggestions. One is that the balconies of multistory apartment buildings could be made a bit deeper. Laundry and *futon*s could then be hung where they would be hidden by the floor and railing from the sight of those below. The other idea is to make balconies larger to promote them as ''apartment gardens,'' something which could be quite a boon for enjoying the dwelling. While freestanding dwellings are often hidden from view by trees and hedges, it is necessary to give more thought to the planning process which will create a distinction between front and rear.

One more factor will have to be considered in developing any positive policy to solve the problem. That is the psychological impact of washing/drying activities in Japan. One suggestion would be to dry laundry or *futon*s in a more aesthetically attractive manner. For example, all clothing of a given type could be hung together, so that regular row patterns are created. And sleeping *futon*s could be purchased, with an eye to how they would look airing on the balcony. Instead of buying fine-grained patterns, one would consider colors and shapes as they will appear from afar. For example if the *futon*s are all the same color, even if it is a primary color, they would not look bad no matter how many of them were set out together. Some sort of geometric pattern on them could also be attractive. The *futon* could then become a design which is conceived as a sort of tapestry or wall hanging.

As farfetched as this idea may appear on the surface, it echoes problems that modern western architects have tackled when building apartment complexes and office buildings. They make a conscious attempt to unify the color of window dressing as viewed from the outside. In order to do this they offer the new occupants two-toned blinds or curtains, with a standardized color on the outside and a free choice of color on the inside.

This idea of drying things attractively is worth some attention. If the daily laundry chore has an aspect of enjoyment, and if the Japanese take pleasure in "wearing the sunlight," then rather than encouraging the use of dryers, it would not be unreasonable to encourage the Japanese to incorporate more attractive clothes-drying procedures. If this comes about, perhaps the day will come when architects need not be in any hurry to photograph their work.

Basements

When it comes to structures built below the surface of the earth, Japan and the West find themselves in exactly opposite positions.

Some claim that Japan is more developed than the West in terms of utilizing underground space. They cite such examples as the vast basement food markets which characterize Japanese department stores, the arrays of restaurants and bars in the basements of office buildings and the extensive underground malls around central train terminals. Indeed, many millions of urban Japanese take these structures for granted, while tourists on their first visits to Japan find them astonishing. In a western city it is rare to come across a building with a basement eating and drinking complex, and even rarer to find an underground shopping mall. In the 1950s, a large underground mall was built around the central station in Stockholm, but it turned out to

An underground shopping area in Shinjuku Ward, Tokyo.

Shosoin: a raised storehouse dating from the 8th century
in which priceless artifacts were stored.

be rather unpopular. The main reason why people wouldn't come to it
was that the space was cut off from sunlight. But Japan is another story.
Looking at the bustling crowds in a brightly lit underground mall can
lead to the conclusion that Japan has a very strongly developed "basement culture."

On the other hand, while the typical western home often includes a
basement, in Japan a home with a basement is unusual. In this sense, it
appears that the utilization of underground residential space in Japan
has not yet become popular.

The Japanese approach to the utilization of underground space is
very different from that of the other highly developed nations of the
world. This basically resulted from differences in climatic and geolo-
gical conditions.

There is no tradition of building into the ground in Japan. This is because the country has a very humid climate and high water tables. Consequently, flooring of a wooden dwelling is required by law to be placed at least 45 centimeters (18 inches) above the ground. If this is not done, the wooden foundation and supporting posts will quickly rot away. Yet even that regulation does not dispose of humidity as a household problem. Unless there is constant ventilation, excessive humidity within a range of one to one-and-a-half meters (3.3 to 5 feet) above the ground will soon cause clothing in dresser drawers to become moldy. Consequently, the Japanese have traditionally stored their important possessions either in a separate storehouse structure or in an atticlike space near the roof of the home. The humidity of an underground space is even worse, especially where ventilation is poor.

In such cases storage underground is completely out of the question.

These factors have contributed to the traditional belief that the area below the ground is the realm of the dead. The living were loath to enter an area where objects quickly decomposed. This is another reason why basements were virtually non-existent in Japan until the Meiji period (1868–1912). The only exceptions were the small cellars with which some ordinary homes were furnished in the medieval and modern eras, and an underground prison in Edo (now Tokyo) during the Edo period (1603–1867). The former were used only as places to store the household possessions to protect them in case of fire, while the latter housed mainly criminals who were condemned to death.

In Europe, by way of contrast, where the climate is generally rather dry and the water tables below cities tend to be low, basement rooms are common and mold is not usually much of a problem. And since the ambient temperature of the underground space remains more or less constant throughout the year, the basement has become indispensable in the ordinary home as a food storage area. In this respect the western basement may be thought of as the equivalent of the Japanese storehouse. It is only natural, then, that the houses of European farmers and city dwellers alike have basements. The wine industry in particular utilizes very large cellars for aging wines. In this respect, underground space can be said to have made a major contribution to European culture.

In spite of the severe natural constraints, the use of underground space has steadily developed in Japan during the past century, thanks to advances in construction technology. With the advent of steel-reinforced concrete, it became possible to build structures underground with materials which are nearly invulnerable to decomposition. The improvement of waterproofing techniques, based on the use of such substances as asphalt, made underground construction relatively easy, despite the high water tables. Accordingly, since the Japanese always tend to seek even just a bit more space, basements have become a standard feature of the modern building. The soft soil of Japan turned out to be an advantage because it is relatively easy to sink the necessary bearing piles some 20 or 30 meters into the earth to reach bedrock in order to provide stability for standard concrete buildings. It is also relatively easy to replace the soft soil with basement space. These factors promoted the rapid development and diffusion of basement construction. Nowadays the notion that the area below ground level is the domain of the dead seems about as current as the theory that the earth is flat.

Yet one stumbling block remains. Although it is possible to prevent the building from rotting away due to humidity and to prevent ground-water from permeating the structure, the problem of moisture in the air has still not been completely solved. This is why most of the basement spaces constructed in Japan before World War II were dank, dismal and moldy-smelling places.

After World War II, there was rapid development of ventilation equipment and technologies for artificially controlling the basement atmosphere. But the elimination of humidity with mechanical ventilation is difficult to accomplish in a really thorough manner. Because it is too expensive to keep the ventilating equipment running twenty-four hours a day, plans for long-term storage in basements have generally been unsuccessful. The most conspicuous successes among Japanese basements are the department store food floors, but, of course, these spaces are entirely devoted to food retailing. Long-term damage from humidity is not a problem to either the fast-moving perishables or to long-lasting canned goods. Department store basements were formerly used to market such products as watches or clothing, and moisture-related damage was common. Nowadays most stores give the basement over entirely to food retailing. Furthermore, the basements in almost every new office building are filled with coffee shops and restaurants. These are examples of successful utilization of basement space, supported by the use of modern ventilation and refrigeration equipment. But people are actually only present in these places during a fixed period of the day. If the ventilation and temperature control equipment had to be run day and night, it would be prohibitively expensive to operate and maintain.

Thus we can understand the difficulties involved in underground storage of goods which are sensitive to humidity. The current fashion for underground parking lots is an example which is in the phase of being tested by society. Since automobiles and other types of machinery are quite liable to be damaged by moisture, it is not desirable to leave cars underground for long periods of time. Machinery in rooms located in basements have shown deterioration due to humidity, and the trend now is to place various types of equipment on the roof. Since this is the case in commercial buildings, it hardly needs to be said that in the average house it would be unthinkable to furnish a basement with ventilation equipment. The Japanese still need to grapple with the problem of using basement space, including such issues as mass shelters in times of disaster.

Large buildings in Europe, by the way, seldom have basements. One reason is, as said before, Europeans hold the firmly rooted notion that underground spaces which do not receive any sunlight are not fit for human habitation. A basement is the setting for Maksim Gorky's (1868–1936) play *The Lower Depths* (1906), which describes in detail the dismal life of a band of revolutionaries who have eluded the authorities. There is a strong consciousness in Europe that a basement is a place for things, for storage, and is not a living space. Another problem rises out of environmental limitations: European cities, especially the central districts, are mostly located on top of major rock formations. Consequently, large-scale underground construction tends to be very difficult. This can affect homes as well. In Stockholm, for example, it is not uncommon for a natural outcropping to be utilized as a wall of a house, rather like a cellar.

To sum up, in both Japan and in Europe people have always felt that underground spaces were not fit for human habitation, but for different reasons. In Japan, people believed things kept underground would mildew, and in Europe people felt basements were dark and gloomy places. Nonetheless, Europeans have long made effective use of basements, not as living spaces but as storage areas, whereas the Japanese could not do so because of climatic conditions or architectural limitations. As soon as the Japanese obtained technology which made it possible to utilize the additional space, the taboo was quickly abandoned and people began to use basements for human activities. Underground storage is still not feasible in private residences in Japan because objects cannot adapt to environments the way people do. Some recent house designs in England and America have used half-basements as family rooms, dens or studies, but even with proper ventilation this application is not likely to catch on in Japan. It seems that if viable half-basements were to be developed in Japan, their use would be rather limited.

If I may be forgiven for talking of my own home, we once got to the stage of holding a family meeting to decide whether or not to include a half-basement in the plans for extending our house. Nobody had any brilliant ideas for solving the humidity problem, but one suggestion that came up was to build a game room for a Ping-Pong table. Since the public athletic facilities are always crowded, we all thought that was a fine idea. But in the end we found we just couldn't afford the space, and it remained a dream.

It seems to me that the Japanese are not yet ready to decide how to use a residential basement.

Storage

Japan has been talking about its "housing shortage" for so long that the phrase "*jutaku nan*" has entered the dictionaries, yet no solution seems to be in sight. The discussion has quieted down in recent years, as if we have collectively given up. In the bookstores today there are plenty of books about the "city of the future," but very few about the housing shortage.

The housing shortage is one problem that won't go away. Local governments and public housing corporations have been building some 200,000 units per year, and loans from the national government have enabled the construction of another 500,000 or so homes each year. With the activities of the private sector contributing an equal or greater number of units, the total is extremely high figure for a capitalist country. The proportion of Japan's gross national product which is devoted to housing investment is approximately seven percent. Considering that this is about twice the average proportion spent on housing investment in the world's other capitalist nations, Japan is indeed devoting large sums of money to housing construction every year.

Between 1948 and 1988, a total of 28 million houses were erected. Adding the 14 million homes which existed at the end of the war, we reach a total of about 42 million. After adjustment for houses which were razed for new construction or destroyed by fire, there are 38 million homes at present in the country. On the face of it, this figure seems to be adequate for the 121 million people of Japan, who make up about 37 million households.

With this much housing stock on hand, what is this housing shortage that has figured so strongly in the national consciousness for several decades?

There are two basic problems contributing to the housing shortage.

One is that there is not sufficient space in which to build the number of required homes. Japan is still in an era of urbanization, with people continually moving to the cities, but we haven't caught up in distributing the housing supply to respond to this urban concentration. The result is that while in the city there are cases where a family of five may live in a single four-and-a-half-mat room (about 8 square meters, or 86 square feet), in the countryside it is not so rare to see a spacious old home occupied only by an elderly grandmother. In other words, the housing supply does not match regional demand, and the statistics are not accurately adjusted to reflect that demand. The housing problem can be excused to some extent on the grounds that the avalanche of people moving to the cities was too massive for instant solutions. But that doesn't solve the problem.

The other problem has to do with those houses which have been built. Here is a story which I heard recently from an elderly couple. When their son and daughter formed households of their own and moved out, the parents expected their house to become a bit roomier, but somehow it seemed just as cramped as ever. The reason was that when the kids got their own places, they left many of their possessions behind due to lack of space in their new places. The parents felt that they couldn't move the things out of their children's old bedrooms without permission, so they left the rooms intact. Even after the son and daughter had married, they wouldn't allow the parents to lay a finger on their belongings. Instead they brought over some of their new possessions. In winter they would store the summer *futon*s, fans and screen doors, and in summer they would arrive with their cars full of kerosene stoves and winter *futon*s and so forth to exchange them for the summer goods. When they had babies, the beds and sofas were in the way, so they asked if they could leave them at the parents' home for a while. As the children grew, the baby carriages and bath basins and tricycles were brought over to store for a while. Later, desks and bookcases, bicycles and even pianos went back and forth from house to house. "Our house turned into the kids' storeroom," the grandparents complained. And it didn't stop there. During summer vacation or spring break, the son and daughter would bring their families for extended visits, during which the house would be bursting at the seams. The old folks could barely find room to sit down. Eventually they found some relief by adding a room on to the house.

If the son and daughter move out, leaving the parents alone in the house, something must be wrong if an addition has to be built. Such cases aren't found in the home economics textbooks. The conventional view is that a small home is fine for an elderly couple. But we have seen that in reality that is not necessarily true.

That couple's experience may have been an extreme example, but the fact is that similar stories can be heard all over Japan. Of course, part of the problem is the development of the nuclear family. When separate households are established, it is largely a matter of appearance, for parents and children still remain bound by strong emotional ties. There is even some reason to think that the traditional conflict between daughter-in-law and mother-in-law—once a salient feature of the typical Japanese household—has disappeared, and family ties have thus become stronger. Which is to say that the breakup of the traditional ex-tended-family household has improved the intra-familial relationships.

The other reason behind this pattern is of course the structure of the urban homes that the son and daughter are living in. Whether it is in public housing or a private apartment, chances are very good that a couple's "starter" residence is very, very small. There are few rooms, and the dimensions of each room are extremely small. But the most in-convenient thing is that there is very little storage space. This is what created the situation previously described.

Having analyzed the situation to this extent, let us tackle the problem of storage. It is clear that new Japanese homes don't have space in which to put things away. This was not always the case. In the old days, large homes had separate storehouses, and small homes had attics or *tsushi* (unfinished second stories). In contemporary homes not only are there no storehouses, but the designs do not provide closet or attic space or even space above the beams which can be used for storage. Mean-while, all sorts of electrical and electronic equipment, household goods and consumer products have been put on the market. People buy them, even though they may have no place to arrange them nicely in their homes.

Recently built homes in Europe and America tend to have basements devoted to storage space which account for nearly half of the total area of the dwelling. In apartment buildings, the occupants have access to either joint storage areas or to private storage rooms in the basement. In Japan, basement storage is not feasible, mainly because of climatic con-ditions. This odd and often invisible disparity is actually quite large. In international comparisons of dwelling sizes, the storage area is not usu-ally included in the calculation of the floor area of a western home, which makes the figure meaningless. We normally hear that in com-parison with a Japanese house, a European house has about two times the area and an American house three times the area, whereas if the

A series of traditional storehouses along the Sayo River, Hyogo Prefecture.

storage space is included in the calculation, the true figures would likely be three times and five times the area, respectively.

Actually, Japanese people used to take storage space very seriously in their houses. If we compare the traditional homes of Europe and Japan on the basis of how things were kept, we find that the western home has what might be called a "museum pattern" and the Japanese home a "theater pattern." In the western home, a series of sideboards and other pieces of furniture are placed in the rooms for the purpose of keeping things other than emergency food stores. The halls and living rooms of a conventional middle-class home in the West are fitted out much like a museum, with portraits and sculptures, guns and hunting trophies, painted plates and the like lining the walls, and all manner of china and silver are arranged and displayed in glazed china cabinets. What a contrast this is to the traditional Japanese sitting room in which nothing is displayed aside from a hanging scroll and perhaps a pot with some flowers! Most of the time, not even seating cushions are left on the floor. When guests are due, the cushions and perhaps a dining table and food service are brought out from the storage area. Otherwise, the sitting room remains empty, quite like the stage of a theater. According to the progression of the scenes, sets and props are brought out from the wings and spread around the stage. The decorations, which almost always consist of a scroll and vase of arranged flowers in the alcove, are changed from time to time according to the season.

Since everyday living space is a theater stage, a room corresponding to the prop room where the sets are kept is required. Without such a space, the Japanese living quarters are thrown into disorder. The main constituent of the floor of the Japanese living space, the tatami mat, was not originally designed or constructed for furniture to be placed on it. Rather, it is more like a "modified bed" designed to cushion the human body and to provide a soft sensation. Placing a dresser, desk, bookcase, piano or other piece of heavy furniture on top of it creates dents in the tatami as well as irregular coloration due to lack of exposure to sun and air. The size of the traditional room is closely related to the tatami mat, and furthermore the assumption was made that furniture would not be placed upon the tatami. If the room is indiscriminately filled up with furniture and appliances, as often happens out of necessity, the already small space becomes smaller and smaller.

Nowadays in Japan there is much talk of "the art of arranging." This is a natural outgrowth of the confusion that has arisen as the western style of displaying objects is being grafted onto the traditional Japanese residence. When the two styles are combined, it inevitably results in the building of homes without storage space.

Meanwhile, in Europe, where there is no lack of storage space, there is a contemporary trend in interior design toward the simplicity that formerly characterized the Japanese home. It is especially visible in Scandinavia, Germany and Italy. To a degree, East and West are exchanging traditions.

The contemporary Japanese home, with its lack of storage space, is simply an incomplete residence. No matter how many homes are mass-produced, this type of design will never lead to a solution of the housing shortage. The problem of storage is particularly compelling in spurring us to examine the direction in which the Japanese dwelling in general is heading.

Eaves

A few years back, weather patterns all over the planet seemed to be going haywire. One year Moscow would report a mild winter with springlike weather, and the next we would hear about October snows in Africa, and so forth. In Japan, the newspapers were full of stories of the Weather Bureau predicting a "mild winter" or a "long spell of clear weather." But with all of the various fluctuations, one thing never did seem to change: Japan remained a rainy place. I recall one summer when Paris suffered from unusually heavy rainfall, and tourists were quite inconvenienced. The newspapers presented the details, and reported that the total monthly rainfall during July reached some 20 millimeters (0.79 inches). That is an amount that might fall in an hour during a severe cloudburst of the sort with which anyone who has spent a summer in Japan is familiar. The Parisians may well have thought they were having heavy rainfall, but to a Japanese it didn't seem like much of a problem.

Contemporary Japanese culture doesn't think so much about rain anymore. King Faisal of Saudi Arabia once remarked while visiting Japan, "In Japan there is rain, and in my country there is oil." The newspaper reporters who were present wrote some interesting stories, but I wonder how many of us understood the true significance of his words.

It's hardly necessary to check the map to realize that most of the world's civilizations developed on the continental land masses. One ancient exception was the island culture in the Aegean Sea centered on Crete, but it was not able to achieve historical permanence. Yet there is a group of four islands in the Pacific Ocean, which today stands with Great Britain as one of the two island nations of the world at the apex of modern civilization. If the Japanese archipelago lay in an arid zone

Projecting eaves offer increased rain protection for this farmhouse.

with little rain, its mountains would not be able to support forests. Moreover, Japan would only be able to harvest meager crops of rice. Both the appearance of the country and the structure of its society would be entirely different.

It is precisely because rain is such a heavenly blessing that it has never been something which farmers disliked. If it were, they could hardly have been successful. They donned bamboo hats and straw raincoats and worked in the rain. Despite living in such a rainy climate, the farmers of ancient Japan did not have umbrellas.

While gratefully extending both hands to receive the blessing of rain, even in ancient times the farmers made meticulous preparations to protect themselves from it. An example is the structure of the ancient pit dwellings. These houses had the appearance of roofs set on the ground. People would go in and out through slits cut into the sloping roofs.

The shape of a roof not only affected the individual structure, but it could also affect the overall design of a city, as illustrated by this description of the appearance of Edo (now Tokyo) found in *Sora-oboe*:

> The eaves of the shops running along the public passageways, called *inubashiri*, on both sides to the service entrances, are the routes from one end of town to the other.

The *inubashiri* was a type of berm or passageway made of stones or tiles cemented together with lime, which was placed around the perimeter of a building at ground level. In order to protect house foundations against moisture, the foundations were commonly surrounded by such berms, hardened with some sort of cement, measuring about 5 to 10 centimeters (2 to 4 inches) in depth and 30 to 40 centimeters (1 foot to 1.3 feet) in width. *Inubashiri* transliterates as ''dog run,'' and it was just wide enough to serve as such, but in fact during the Edo period (1603–1867) people walked along them. The *inubashiri*, protected by the eaves projecting from the roof of each townhouse and from the front of each shop, were open to the public and served as the town's pedestrian traffic routes. Such was the original pattern of the space under the eaves of townhouses:

> When the city of Edo was originally laid out, the avenues were made 10 *ken* [about 18 meters, or 60 feet] wide, with an area eight *ken* [14.4 meters, or 48 feet] wide in the center for public street traffic, set off on both sides by water ditches. Between the ditches and the homes were *inubashiri* one *ken* [1.8 meters, or 6 feet] wide. Although they were not private property, eaves or canopies over-

A modified *inubashiri* (or *gangi*), often found in snowy regions.

hung them. When it rained, these protected footpaths served the homes and shops by providing shelter for guests and customers.

The description continues for the Meiji period (1868–1912):

Under the reforms of the Meiji period, the *inubashiri* were transferred to the private landholdings, and the avenues which were previously 10 *ken* [18 meters, or 60 feet] in width were reduced to the present eight *ken* [14 meters, or 48 feet].

This is something which should not be overlooked. A house site is on privately held land, subject to taxation, which extends up to the edge of the street. But the *inubashiri* were public rights of way, and not private land. Being one *ken* in width, these provided excellent public passages. In fact they were sidewalks, and they were used as such from the time they were first constructed. This is why they were paved with stone or tile. The homeowners were allowed to project eaves or canopies out over the *inubashiri*. This was done out of consideration for pedestrians and customers, but at the same time it prevented the land under the eaves from standing idle. In Japanese architecture, greatly extended eaves were necessary to provide protection from the rain. If the eaves had not been allowed to project above the public right of way, the house would have had to be set back a greater distance, corresponding to the

149

Inuyarai, dog fences, abut this traditional townhouse. Despite their name, these fences were primarily aimed at preventing people rather than dogs from getting too close to the house.

space between the wall of the building and the outer edge of the eaves. Thus the land available to the private landowner would have been that much smaller. To expand their land size, landowners were permitted to extend eaves or canopies out over the public rights of way, but only over the *inubashiri* passageways. In the Meiji period, these passages were transferred to the private landholdings since they were covered by the eaves of the private homes.

The resulting forms can still be seen in downtown neighborhoods of Kyoto, where the strip of land under the eaves of a home is often surrounded by a fence, or covered with strips of bamboo arching from the street to a point on the wall about one meter (3.3 feet) above the ground (both of which carry the interchangable names *inuyarai*, ''dog fence,'' or *komayose*, ''horse barrier''). Calling such barriers ''dog fences'' or "house barriers" keeps up the pretense of politeness, while in fact they serve quite well as "human fences." Also, at the boundaries between houses, the *inubashiri* strip is frequently divided by *sodekabe* ("wing walls"), which may be made of wooden storm doors or masonry blocks or whatever material happens to be available. Like *udatsu* (the roof wall separating two houses, especially units of row houses), these serve as defense against fire, but they also happen to frustrate passersby who might otherwise be inclined to walk down the covered *inubashiri* strip. This is where the role of the *inubashiri* as a passageway comes completely to an end. Further, exterior lattices or bay windows have often been installed above the *inubashiri*. Even worse, sometimes wooden doors are put up around half of the *inubashiri* area, and it becomes an extension of the interior space of the house. A walk through the downtown Kyoto neighborhoods indicates just how far these changes have progressed. Of course this is not something which is limited only to Kyoto. But in other large Japanese cities, especially in Tokyo and Osaka, there are almost no old houses left, so it is natural to dwell on the example of Kyoto.

Two factors helped create the environment in which this sort of privatization of the public right of way, which we might call "socially larcenous behavior," was possible. One is the confusion which reigned after the fall of the shogunate in 1867, and the other is the ideal of private property which came from Europe a short time later and was enshrined in modern civil law. The way of thinking which holds that "Proprietary rights in land extend above and below the land" (Article 207, Civil Code) dictates a clear answer as to whether the land below the eaves is public or private space. The earlier common law of Japan had concentrated on the benefits accruing from land, while land ownership tended to be not so clearly specified. Through the wave of modernization, spaces such as the *inubashiri* which were of mixed public and private use in accordance with the previous common law were quickly confiscated for private profit.

As a result many Japanese streets became much narrower and lost their rain shelter, so that moving along them in the rain became somewhat inconvenient. The eaves-shaded passageway, an outstanding piece of urban design which was born out of the culture of a rainy country in which people could keep out of the rain by passing under the eaves of houses, will very soon disappear from the contemporary Japanese city. These days one can't just open one's umbrella and calmly walk along without some driver honking crazily from behind.

The present-day culture of Japan is becoming weaker and weaker with respect to rain. When a heavy rainstorm comes along, the national railways become snarled and accidents occur due to flooding. Moreover, everyday life in the city becomes extremely unpleasant because of the rain. During a sudden cloudburst, cars zoom by, splashing water on us, the footpaths become dangerously slippery, people struggle to catch taxis and the buses turn into steambaths. For children and the elderly, a rainy day in the city can be a hellish torment.

Time was when the Japanese very cleverly protected themselves from rain, with long overhanging eaves and raised sidewalks stretching into every nook and corner of the towns. Long overhanging eaves are frequently cited as a special feature of Japanese architecture and as a beautiful design detail. They were not meant merely to be attached to individual structures here and there, but rather also to be socially useful. For example, they were meeting places, for chance encounters would often occur among strangers taking shelter from the rain under the eaves. Sometimes love affairs began there. In fact it was a public space that could function almost like a plaza. This sort of "culture of rain" has now been choked off. What we find instead are the covered sidewalks and streets of shopping arcades, but these are not the same as the old overhanging eaves and raised sidewalk spaces which provided shelter throughout the city.

I don't know if it is in step with the above trend or not, but the overhangs of the ordinary home have been gradually shrinking from the original 90 centimeters (3 feet) down to 75 or 60 or even 45 centimeters (30, 24 or even 18 inches). The extended eaves, which were long a hallmark of Japanese architecture, are shrinking because they have lost their social function. Their other specific characteristics are also withering away.

Verandas

The Japanese words for "veranda" or "porch" are based on the character meaning "edge" or "margin," and yet it can be a very important element of the house. It does little to make the house larger in a physical sense, but in a psychological sense it can eliminate the feeling of smallness. One of the best features of a Japanese house is the sense of contentment and communion with nature one can have by looking at the garden through the half-glazed sliding doors of the sitting room and the glazed sliding doors of the veranda. When the doors on both sides of the veranda are opened, the "edge" is bridged and a continuous space is formed between the sitting room and the garden. Lying on the porch on a summer afternoon in a cool breeze, growing more and more sleepy, one gets the same sort of feeling as if taking a nap in the shade of a tree in the garden. In other words, the veranda is more or less the same as the garden.

The odd thing about a Japanese veranda, about this space on the edge, with an open space under the eaves for instance, is that it is not clear whether it is an interior space or an exterior space. Viewed from inside, an open veranda, with its glazed sliding doors exposed to the wind, seems to be an exterior space. But seen from the outside, with its wooden floor and roof or canopy formed by the eaves, it is difficult to consider the veranda a purely outdoor space. Even if it is not really a part of the interior of the structure, it can be considered an attached space. From the point of view of architectural composition, it is perhaps an arbor in the garden which has a roof but no walls, or maybe it is an open space with walls but no roof. No matter how we look at it, it is some sort of "half-structure" from which some element is missing.

Also, a veranda which lies within glass sliding doors does not have a ceiling such as a regular sitting room would, but instead the underside

A typical farmhouse veranda.

of the eaves is normally left exposed. Which is to say that in the context of Japanese architecture, this is not an interior space. In the old days before glass sliding doors existed, except for occasions such as typhoons or blizzards when shutters would be set in from the outside, most verandas were simply left exposed to the wind. In the countryside many farmhouses with such verandas can still be seen today.

This strange space which is neither indoors nor outdoors is considered by some architects to be unclassifiable without its own label as a "connecting space" or "third space."

An old lady in my neighborhood lives in a western-style house which her son and daughter-in-law had built for her, the type of home that the Japanese call "modern style." It doesn't have a veranda. In the old days, she says, every house had a veranda. The old folks could spend the whole day sitting on the veranda doing their needlework, watching their grandchildren or maybe stepping out into the garden and back into the house. What's more, sitting on the veranda you could see the people passing by and what they were doing. You could exchange greetings with the neighbors. Sometimes they would even come up and sit on the veranda for a chat. When it rained you could just close the sliding doors, and when the weather was pleasant you could just sit there and take a nap.

For an old person, the veranda is a secure, pleasant place. If a veranda is excluded from a new house, then no matter how modern the design, for the elderly it would be an inconvenient and dreary home. One might suggest that they can always go outside, but even to step out to the local park a Japanese woman usually wants to change her clothes. Going out for a walk is not such a casual thing. Unlike the old days, the streets are full of cars and therefore somewhat fearsome. The thought of having to cross a footbridge can also be rather disconcerting. My neighbor's son bought her a television to make indoor living easier, but of course she can't have a conversation with a television. All in all, she seems rather lonely.

This is something that the Japanese really need to reconsider. What does today's culture hold for senior citizens? At the least we can say that the Japanese version of the "American modern home," which excludes the veranda, is not a welcome development. This applies not only to the elderly. For housewives, for small children and for working men on their days off, a veranda adjoining the garden is uplifting. Life in contemporary Japanese homes without verandas has clearly become a notch more insipid.

The Japanese word for veranda came originally from the word "*fuchi*" for "hem," and referred specifically to the decorative edging of the cuffs or hems of ancient Chinese clothing. There were several reasons for adding edging to cuffs and hems. One reason was to prevent the threads of the clothing from unraveling. Secondly, it was to reinforce frayed sections on the edge of the garment. Sometimes a new piece was attached in place of the frayed part, so that the term had the significance of a tatami mat, which in fact is considered a replaceable item. The third reason was, of course, decoration, for the ancient hems were usually referred to as decorative hems. Tatami edging was also more decorative in former times than today, with various figured patterns being used.

A typical Shinto shrine veranda. Usa jingu.

These concepts of edging in clothing and tatami can also be applied to the Japanese house. Which is to say that the veranda (in Japanese, "the edge" or "the edge-side") serves as a reinforcement of the perimeter of a house which is constructed from, besides wood, the soft materials of paper and especially tatami mats. Without the veranda at the rim of the structure, the interior space of the open-plan Japanese house could be directly penetrated by rain and sunlight, and the tatami and sliding paper doors and earthen walls would suffer significant damage. Given that the Japanese home is made from soft materials and has an open plan, the veranda rim becomes something which is in a physical sense an indispensable element of the structure. In addition, it is important as a "recreational space." While the sitting rooms are areas restricted by traditional etiquette and social rank, the veranda is a free space not bound by social rules of status. Since the veranda doesn't have the alcove with its formal, mood-setting scroll, there is no sense of seniority or inferiority in this area. Here people can relax freely before or after having a meal in the sitting room.

With these points in mind, we find that the veranda of the Japanese house takes on unexpected significance in terms of both architectural structure and of living activities. The western veranda or balcony may be considered similar in these respects, yet it is not comparable in openness to the Japanese veranda which is enclosed by sliding glass or glass and paper doors. The word "balcony" derives from the Italian crenellated boxlike structure called a *balcone*. Italianate porticos and colonnades bear formal resemblance to the Japanese veranda, but they do not work as well to provide continuity between the interior space and the outdoor garden.

The history of the veranda goes far back in Japanese architecture. All the various types of Shinto shrine structures, which basically retain the features of the ancient *miya*, or aristocratic palaces, are surrounded by verandas with railings. It is unclear whether the raised-floor dwelling originally had a veranda, but extant bronze mirrors depict buildings from the Tumulus period (4th–7th centuries) with balconylike structures. Later, in the *shinden* style of the Heian period (794–1185), verandas with slatted wooden or bamboo floors were fitted around the structures. These correspond to the present-day open veranda. On the other hand, one of the distinctive features of the *shinden*-style aristocratic residence, the long, narrow spaces which formed a concentric ring around the central building and which were known as various types of eaves or overhangs, corresponds to the contemporary enclosed veranda. Thus the veranda may well have developed as a structurally or functionally indispensable outer element of the open-plan house which incorporated the earlier raised-floor dwelling style.

Having inherited such a tradition, it is well for the Japanese to broaden the ideal of the balcony in their homes to include, for example, open-plan balconies in front of the windows of apartments or office buildings. This adds charm to life.

The veranda is one of several types of traditional living spaces which were fostered by the climate and society of Japan over many centuries, and which are being thoughtlessly abandoned as "old-fashioned" by the new mechanistic culture. Unfortunately, the charm and livability which the veranda has traditionally provided are in increasingly shorter supply in the common houses of today's Japan.

Shinden-style verandas. Phoenix Hall, Byodoin, 11th century.

Detail of hall's far-left veranda.

Gardens

The Japanese love gardens. This is not only a typical comment of foreigners, but also something which the Japanese themselves believe. But is this really the case? There are indeed countless examples of temples and historic sites with gardens which have been cited as master-pieces. There are even nameless buildings with gardens worthy of designation as National Treasures. The miniature *tsubo* gardens which are painstakingly created behind traditional townhouses are, no matter how cramped the space, works of elegant and subtle beauty. But these are mostly things of the past.

Among the rows and rows of ready-built homes with multicolored tile roofs which are steadily being erected in suburban districts, one seldom encounters anything resembling a proper Japanese garden of arranged rocks and shrubs. But it is not only ready-built homes that don't have proper Japanese gardens. Even when architects set aside a proper space for a garden for a detached home built to order on a real estate lot, the garden tends to gradually disappear after a few years as an extra room is added or the space is put to some other, more practical use. In the case of an old house which is still standing, one can say with certainty that it has a garden, whereas for a recently erected ordinary house this can no longer be said.

Of course, it can be said that the reason for this is that land prices have escalated and as a result the affordable lot has become smaller and smaller. Yet while the garden tends to be disappearing, one of the most visible features of the new home is that it has a car or a garage sitting next to it. This is equally true for detached homes, row houses and ren-tal homes. While the front yard or entry approach to a detached home is likely to have been given over to the automobile, what one usually finds in the case of a ready-built row house is that not only is the front yard a

Former garden turned into a parking space.

parking space, but the tiny rear garden is the only area in which to dry clothes. With land prices going through the roof, overnight parking prohibited because of the narrowness of the streets, and the difficulty of renting parking spaces, people have cast about for someplace to put the car, and they have used whatever space that could be found. The result, ironic though it may seem, is that the garden has been turned into a garage. Viewing a modern residential area, one might well comment that the Japanese have changed from a garden-loving people to an automobile-loving people.

That the automobile has become a necessity of life in today's society is a fact which has to be recognized. People haven't converted their gardens to garages for the fun of it. The housing circumstances of our time have operated to force us to the point where this has become necessary, and this should give us pause for thought.

How is it that this love for the garden, which has supposedly been lodged profoundly in the hearts of the Japanese for hundreds of years, can so easily be extinguished for the sake of a single modern convenience which has only recently appeared on the scene? Could there possibly be something amiss with the cherished idea that the Japanese love gardens?

From ancient times it has often been said that the garden is a ''work of art'' which is to be appreciated while sitting in the drawing room. Thus the garden is something to be seen, and not a place to exercise in or to relax in. Most older Japanese, those who were raised before the war, are likely to have memories of being scolded by their mothers on this score: "Get out of there. The garden is not a place for playing!" On this point there is a wide disparity between the western notion that the garden or yard is a place for outdoor enjoyment and the idea that a garden is to be looked at. It may have been exactly this idea of the garden as a "work of art" or "luxury item" that, with the arrival of the "necessity" known as the automobile, created the rapid demise of the garden. After the addition of a new room for the children and the construction of a garage, the last remaining space in the garden is usually used to hang out the laundry. After all, necessities of life such as a car and clean clothes simply cannot be ignored.

How, then, did the difference arise between a "viewing garden" and a "doing garden"? To answer this we have to look at the respective origins of the western and the Japanese garden or, if you will, at the two opposing poles of thought from which they have sprung.

On the European side, if we start with the garden which is an adjunct to the home, we have the patio or courtyard. This developed originally as a square-shaped space in the center of the building which served both to admit light and as a central passageway, thus it somewhat resembled the tiny *tsubo* garden of Japan. The fundamental difference of course is that the courtyard is a space for human activity, while the *tsubo* garden is for purely visual enjoyment. In a manner of speaking, the courtyard is a hall without a roof.

Aside from this private sort of garden, the Europeans also have public gardens or parks. A distinctive characteristic of the garden in European society is that the public park developed further than the private garden.

The character of the European park can be summed up as that of a hunting ground. Even now in English legal usage the word "park" signifies a private game preserve. The origin of the park as a hunting preserve can be traced back to ancient Babylonia. There are records which show that after the hunting people known as the Sumerians came down from the West Asian plateau into the Tigris and Euphrates lowlands and forged an agricultural nation, they created artificial woodlands on the plains and stocked them with wild oxen, deer, goats and the like, which they often hunted.

Later, under the Assyrians, a number of temples and palaces were erected in these game preserves. In Greek civilization, such manmade woodlands evolved from hunting to athletic grounds. Their activities included the quadrennial competitions—the Olympic Games—held in the garden of the Temple of Zeus. Of course the modern European park is never used for hunting, and an athletic ground is likely to be only one of its facilities—if it is present at all. Today among West Asian and European peoples who are descended from hunting cultures, a park tends to call to mind images of the life of old in the woods—hunting and coexisting with animals. Thus small birds and small animals are encouraged to roam freely in the parks. On their days off, people go for walks and feed them. The same sort of thing applies to private gardens. In Europe or the United States, a great many people put out feeders or drinking troughs for birds or small animals—something which is rarely seen in Japan.

"*Niwa*," the Japanese word for garden, originally referred to a large space. For example, the Chronicles of Japan (*Nihonshoki*; 720) tell of the legendary emperor Jimmu ordering that a *matsuri niwa* ("ceremonial ground") be established on a certain mountain. Today among farmers as well as in traditional urban neighborhoods, *niwa* in common speech means a large earthen-floored workspace either inside or out-of-doors, while a proper garden in which trees and plants are cultivated is known by another standard Japanese term (*senzai*).

Then, what did the ancient Japanese call what is today generally known as the *niwa*? The oldest documented garden in Japan, which contained a pond with islands, was constructed by Soga no Umako (?–626) at his home in Asuka. This sort of garden was extremely rare at the time; people thereafter referred to him as "the minister with the island." Later, when Otomo no Tabito (665–731) returned home to the capital at Heijokyo (now Nara) from his post in Kyushu, he wrote this poem:

> In the garden once cultivated by me and my wife,
> How tall and blossom-laden the trees have grown!
> (from the *Manyoshu*, c. A.D. 759, the oldest
> extant collection of Japanese poetry)

Although the term *niwa*, written in an archaic form with characters meaning "house front," can be found in the *Manyoshu* and other texts of the era, this term always referred to the empty land in front of a house. A proper manmade garden, on the other hand, was generally referred to at the time as a *shima* (literally, an island). Literature indicates that this term persisted well into the Heian period (794–1185).

There are grounds for speculating that the use of the word "*shima*" for a garden has some connection with the sea. The Japanese communities of a dozen or so centuries ago were often situated on alluvial plains, near shallow seas with profusions of reeds, or along riverbanks with shifting beds. In such locations, people were accustomed to seeing scattered islands and sandbars. Through the occasional ebbing of the sea level, the sedimentation action of the rivers, and later with the introduction of river control technology from the Asian mainland, new land was gradually created and existing land became more fertile. This is conjecture, but when people moved inland to the plains, might they not have recalled the image of their former island and sandbar haunts, and referred to their own gardens and homesites as *shima*?

> How happy would I be to see
> The sea wash the shore in Suminoe.
> > (*Manyoshu*)

> The island lying off Tamanoura appears in my dream.
> It may come closer to my heart than the shore washed by the sea.
> > (*Manyoshu*)

In ancient poems such as these, we see how the people of the times yearned for the beauties of the seashore and nostalgically recalled their life by the sea.

This may also have been connected to the strongly developed sensitivity for the *furusato* (native place or spiritual home) which is characteristic of the Japanese people.

The question of where the Japanese people came from remains a mystery, but one line of thinking is that they migrated or drifted to Japan from elsewhere, either from the Asian mainland or from the islands of the South Pacific. There are some who hold that some powerful tribe or tribes ''conquered'' Japan. In which case it seems likely that, rather than mounting a direct invasion, they were dislodged by a continental superpower and forced to take temporary refuge in Japan, and their sojourn turned into permanent residence. In such a situation the ''homeland-colony'' relationship between the great mainland power and the settled tribes would have been extremely weak. The majority of these people would have had no ''homeland'' that they could return to. A logical result would be that the Japanese people would forever gaze upon the ocean and fix an ''illusory homeland'' somewhere beyond the sea. Today in Okinawa there is still the concept of the *niraikanai*, the land beyond the sea where the spirits of the ancestors dwell.'' Might this concept not shed light on the spirit of the ancient Japanese?

Indeed, in the *Manyoshu*, gardens were usually depicted as reproductions of seascapes, and this concept was passed on to later eras. A quote

A manmade island in Shugakuin Detached Palace dominates
this garden modeled after a Heian-period archetype.

in what is said to be the world's oldest text on techniques of laying our formal gardens, the *Sakuteiki*, compiled in the 12th century by Tachibana no Toshitsuna, supports this view: "If the rock in the pond is to evoke the sea, its lower part must be marked by waves." The ponds in Japanese gardens have always imitated the sea.

According to a recent residential survey in which I took part, the tree which most Japanese prefer for gardens is the pine. I think that this preference can partly be attributed to the fact that it is the venerable pine that has for centuries withstood the blizzards of the windswept seashore. In the old days as well as now it has evoked the sea in the minds of the Japanese.

If it is indeed the case that the way the Japanese of old made their gardens indicated an urge to return to the sea, then this helps account for the fact that the Japanese garden is a viewing garden. This is because people, especially in former times, had great difficulty moving from place to place because of the sea. Consequently, the sea was to be looked at, not traveled upon. This is how Japanese gardening techniques evolved to produce a spiritually elevated and therefore highly abstract "viewing garden."

In light of all this, we can say that it is no wonder that the Japanese of today, having more or less given up the garden, are considered to have "lost their spiritual foundation."

In order to revive the garden, then, is some sort of spiritual rebirth necessary? What exactly would that entail? Nowadays, through the power of contemporary science, if there is something across the sea, or if something is happening somewhere, we know all about it in detail. For us, there is little of the enigma or mystery which the sea held for people of old. Furthermore, for us there is no question that it is the four islands of Japan which are our homeland. Of course spiritual representation can be freely pursued in things other than the sea, and we should then ask whether it is inevitable that such things be linked with garden making.

Rather than that, I think we should stress the material functions of the garden in contemporary society—trees and shrubs, grass and flowers, birds and insects, the sun, the scents, the wind, and the space. . . . In western Europe on Sunday mornings, one often finds the family assembled on the veranda for breakfast. The Japanese need more room for this sort of living in their gardens and on their apartment balconies.

To give another example, when Westerners find themselves in a yard or in a park on an warm day, they tend to take off their clothes. While

Zen rock garden depicting a sea-scape. Daisen-in, Daitoku-ji.

the Japanese are fastidious about places for "clothes drying," Westerners tend to use their gardens for "people drying." Of course there are climatic differences, but we should envy them their lack of shyness about taking off their clothes. In our case, even in the gardens or on the balconies of our own homes, mature adults are usually too inhibited by fears of what the neighbors might think to sprawl full length in the midday sun, even when fully clothed, and to casually go about eating and talking. This indicates that for the Japanese, the family garden has not yet become a place for relaxation. Whether or not the garden represents the forest or the sea may be beside the point. The fact that it is being used to air laundry and not people shows that despite the talk of democracy, the people of Japan have not come very far in asserting their independence.

Gazebos

W hat kind of neighborhood do you want to live in?'' That was the topic on which junior and senior high school students in a certain Japanese town were asked to write by their youth group. Here is an excerpt from one of the essays:

> The biggest problem that we have is that on rainy days we can't go out and play. Since we can't play, we get irritated. We begin teasing each other and start fighting among ourselves. Therefore we should make *a place like a house* where we can play on rainy days. [Italics added]

In the old days boys would play traditional games and girls would play house under the eaves. But there aren't many houses left anymore with eaves which overhang far enough for that.

In connection with my job, my own house is occasionally overrun by a horde of college students. Rather than coming inside, we sometimes hold a barbecue in the garden. A meal in the garden is quite enjoyable, and a barbecue requires comparatively little effort. It is also inexpensive, although we do of course have to keep an eye on the weather beforehand.

During any season in Japan, one never knows when it may rain; thus it is necessary to take this possibility into account for any outdoor event. The weather is, in fact, unusually changeable in comparison to other parts of the world. In most other countries rainfall tends to be limited to a definite season(s), or to relatively brief squalls. Japan does have a rainy season for about four or five weeks in June and July, but it is by no means the only time when a lengthy rainy period may occur. Throughout Japanese history the arrangements for outdoor events have included alternative sites or dates in case of rainy weather. This even applied in warfare. In the Battle of Okehazama (1560) in Aichi Prefecture, Oda Nobunaga (1534–82) defeated Imagawa Yoshimoto (1519–60) by taking advantage of this custom and mounting a successful surprise attack during a storm. But in today's more highly systematized society, setting alternative dates in case of rain has become less practical. Nowadays a group outing in the rain, with schoolchildren struggling like drowned rats to win team games, is not an uncommon sight.

Being such a rainy country, Japan ought to devote a little more thought to developing "structures for rainy days." Just as the ancient Greeks, whose Mediterranean location was rainless, invented the outdoor plaza, one would expect that the rainy milieu of the Japanese would have led them further toward the development of "outdoor living space." With a little reconsideration of the construction of our cities and dwellings, a rainy day could become not an occasion to be plunged into depression but another enjoyable day.

When the weather turns out to be fine for a formal outdoor occasion, the organizer usually opens his welcoming speech with some remark about being "blessed with splendid weather." But Japan owes her growth and development to the blessing of abundant rain to the point where one might even consider reversing the standard keynote remark. I once attended the wedding of a friend which was held in a small temple on a rainy day. Instead of feeling soaked with perspiration as one might expect, the rain provided a sense of quiet serenity that seemed quite appropriate as the couple embarked on their new life. This left a deep and lasting impression on me.

> In the violet field I spent a night
> Where I came gathering the flowers with delight
>   (*Manyoshu*)

As this ancient poem suggests, the Japanese were once a people given to outdoor life. This is related to the fundamental importance of rice cultivation and various other types of agricultural production.

One type of proof that the Japanese were outdoorsy types is their development of a variety of devices for outdoor use. Farmers, who traversed hill and dale year in and year out, devised raingear from straw and reeds, while townspeople carried large umbrellas and wore various types of wooden *geta* (clogs) with high sole supports. The townspeople also built long overhanging eaves and raised sidewalks. There were also a great many colorful furnishings, devices and decorations which the Japanese traditionally associated with temporary platforms or used directly on the ground to expand the variety of outdoor activities, in-

Benches folded up against the house of a townhouse in Kyoto.

cluding mats made from straw or reeds, red woolen carpets, folding benches placed against a wall (often seen in Kyoto), as well as curtains or bunting placed around a seating or gathering area, nesting picnic boxes, saké kegs with handles, paper lanterns and outdoor stall decorations.

Secondly, indoor activities were relatively simple. The common people thought of a house as little more than something to keep out the rain and the dew. Accordingly, the traditional Japanese house has always faced the garden, that is the outdoors, and has had an extremely open layout, such that the garden is viewed as a part of the house. It would be only slightly sarcastic to invert this view and say that it is the house which is an extension of the outdoor activities, and that it serves basically as a place where one goes for a while in order to sleep.

The evolution from such an outdoor lifestyle toward higher esteem for indoor activities had much to do with the development in Edo-period (1603–1867) *machiya* society of varied entertainment and merry making such as appreciating art objects and holding tea ceremonies in the back rooms of *machiya* townhouses, attending Kabuki and other types of plays in small theaters and enjoying the pleasures of the red-light districts. Meanwhile, yearnings for the outdoor life were expressed in the creation of teahouse architecture patterned after humble country dwellings. Some people were even prompted to hold tea ceremonies in the open air. The changeover to the decisively indoor lifestyle of today occurred because of the influence of western architectural culture. Also influential was the trend, especially since World War II, in which more and more people moved to the cities. As great numbers of steel-reinforced concrete apartments were constructed, children as well as adults came to be shut up inside the new "personal home." In the old days the street in front of the house served as a playground for children as well as an area where adults could socialize, but with the rapid spread of the automobile such outdoor activities gradually became too dangerous.

At any rate, there is in Japanese tradition a special type of structure which was designed to promote outdoor activities, the *azumaya*, or gazebo. The word "*azumaya*" originally meant simply a hipped roof. The word is derived from "*ya*" which refers to a house or building, and "*azuma*" which means "eastern." Gabled roofs, known as *maya*, were often used in the homes of the ruling classes centering around the Yamato court, while the *azumaya*, or hipped roof, was common, beginning with the pit dwellings, among the homes of the ordinary people, especially the lower-class houses of the eastern provinces. The eastern provinces were considered to be the boondocks of Japanese culture until modern times. Today the term has come to signify an earthen-floored building with no walls, open to the winds.

The gazebo came into wide use during the Edo period in tea gardens and in circular landscape gardens that allowed strollers to return to the starting point without revisiting any part of the garden. These were located in the towns, and provided a partial answer to the dreams harbored by urban residents of outdoor life among the fields and mountains. The circular gardens were, as the name suggests, courses laid out around manmade hills and ponds, providing "views" of the mountains and the sea, with gazebos or gazebolike teahouses here and there, as well as fine sites for spreading mats and holding tea ceremonies in the open.

A typical shingled-roof gazebo.

A thatched-roof gazebo.

Shigure-tei, a summer teahouse at Kodai-ji Temple.

Such gazebos are occasionally seen today in parks or gardens. These are structures designed for the particular purpose of providing a pleasant atmosphere. Through the ages various special features have been incorporated into their designs. Being made of unstripped cedar logs, they are typically covered in cedar bark with perhaps a roof mounted on a single log pillar to make an umbrella-like arbor. Benches are arranged in the pattern of an *X* or a swastika (a traditional Buddhist motif). These sorts of designs survive today as the basic pattern for most of the gazebos and pavilions in Japanese parks.

It is my belief that more of these gazebo structures should be provided as public facilities in Japanese cities of today. The bus and trolley stops of European cities are often furnished with gazebolike structures which

Kasa-tei, a summer teahouse at Kodai-ji Temple.

provide the public service of sheltering people from the rain or the hot sun. Lately, there has been a spate of nationwide ''Let's walk'' movements, but no matter how much one may like to walk, human beings occasionally need to pause for a rest. It is necessary to provide benches and rest areas at intervals along the way. Without them it is extremely difficult to make the modern city into a ''walking city.'' This is clearly one area where gazebo-style structures could help in making Japanese cities more ''walkable.''

Next is the home. At this point, to be sure, building a gazebo in the garden of a Japanese home is a bit of a luxurious proposition. That much space is simply unimaginable in the current housing situation. But without going as far as constructing a proper gazebo, the eaves of a house could be extended so that benches could be set against the wall under the overhang. This is an idea adopted from the classical teahouse, which features an outer garden with a waiting chamber that includes a bench. If homes had this sort of facility, where it is possible to have a chat in the garden and where the children can be out of doors on a rainy day, it would be very highly appreciated. Of course other similar types of structures such as terraces, porches or pergolas would work just as well.

Gazebo structures could also be effective enhancers of life if they were built on the grounds of housing developments. Life in the concrete apartment blocks of the city is isolated from nature, and so there is little chance for direct contact with nature. Between the buildings there is usually a fairly large expanse of empty land, but it usually contains nothing more than a playground with a sandbox and swings, the rest being a tasteless space overgrown with grass and weeds. The obvious thing to do is to connect the buildings with a covered corridor (a pergola in the older sense of the word) and improve the green space, making it into a proper garden with a gazebo or an arbor with trained vines (nowadays known also as a pergola) in the middle of it. These steps would not only provide shelter from rain and strong sunlight but would also create pleasant spaces, both open and covered, where people can relax and socialize and which could be used for various other purposes. Contrast this with the yard which is usually found in a public housing project: a dull place which affords no shelter whatever from rain or sun. It is a place which people tend simply to scurry across so that they can once again shut themselves up in their own living spaces.

On the grounds of public housing as well as in the yards of detached homes, there are often carports made of corrugated plastic sheeting placed over metal frames, which on rainy days are apt to be utilized by little girls playing house or engaging in some other activity. There's nothing wrong with children playing in the carport, but how much nicer it would be if more children could take advantage of a wisteria trellis or a gazebo or some other sort of proper summerhouse facility. After all, in former times this ''rainy country'' devised many such fine spaces.

Fences

In discussing Japanese gardening, the noted literary scholar Saisei Muroo (1889–1962), who had many years of experience as a gardener as well as a keen scholarly eye, asserted that the design of the hedge or fence is ultimately the most important.

The new owner of a garden, according to Muroo, will likely concentrate on the trees. The neophyte gardener tries this and that, placing various types of shrubbery in his very own garden until he achieves a fleeting sense of satisfaction. But this activity, driven mainly by a sense of proprietorship, provides the fulfillment he seeks, and he then loses interest. In the words of the 14th-century sage Yoshida Kenko (1283–1350), "many trees in the garden" is a sign of vulgarity. The owner may find satisfaction in possessing a lot of trees, but to the detached observer a garden with an overabundant growth of verdure may well seem a bit artificially tended, or even simply tended for the sake of the tending. It is not so much nouveau riche as petit bourgeois. Before the carefully planted shrubbery has reached its fullest bloom, the attention of the gardener is likely to move on to the next step—the rocks. Unlike the trees, the rocks exhibit little surface change or self-assertion. They are moved hither and thither according to the owner's whim, providing some brief fulfillment of the urge for artistic creation. At some point they are deemed to be placed where they should have been placed, and there is nothing more to be done.

It's not that there is no more to do, but ultimately the very act of tampering with the manmade garden descends to the ridiculous. Instead, Muroo suggests that more pleasure may be found by simply leaving the shrubs and grasses to run riot in their natural state. He contends that going out into the garden from time to time to discover unexpected plants and insects calms the mind through contact with smaller life

A bamboo fence.

forms. This is the attitude of taking more enjoyment from a grove of assorted trees than from a fastidiously tended park. In other words, the essence of the garden lies not in the *sensui* (mountain-and-water) landscaping of an artificial hill but rather in the various trees of nature.

If the shrubbery, flowers and grasses are left to grow without any pruning or tending, Muroo points out that the disposition of the surrounding wall or hedge becomes important. His reasons are (1) within that promiscuous beauty some moderation and tension are required; and (2) when thinking of a garden, even though one's mind is likely to be fascinated by the trees and the rocks, it is actually the enclosing fence or wall, acting as a prop limiting the view of the spectator, which is visually the most impressive. Indeed, for the garden of the average Japanese home, which is confined to a rather diminutive space, that is precisely the case. As long as one takes pains to ensure that the fence, wall or hedge is not discordant with the surroundings, the garden itself can be left untended.

The same applies when one views a home from the street. I once conducted a survey on the scenery of the Sagano area of Kyoto. Aside from the traditional farmhouses and townhouses, I realized from the comments about the ordinary lots—"It looks western," "It looks like ferroconcrete" and so on—that the design of the fence or wall is the most important thing. This is because, quite simply, when the lot is viewed from the street, the first thing the eye is drawn to is the partition between the road and the house. Of course if there is an upper story close to the road, it will also become a major element of the view. How dreary the place would seem if there were no hedge! Especially in the Sagano district, which is noted for its bamboo groves, it is a shame to disrupt the ambience provided by the many bamboo fences. In fact, bamboo, with its beautiful simplicity and straightness, is a good match for modern architecture. In a manner of speaking, although the house design may be a little weak, the overall appearance will be pleasing if the fence is well designed.

An example of this can be seen in the traditional samurai residence. For reasons of status and defense, the warrior's home was usually enclosed by a whitewashed or plain mud wall. Meanwhile, the house itself was of rather humble construction, for the samurai were not a very wealthy class. By way of comparison, the materials used for the posts and beams of a merchant's home in the same town would likely be of very fine quality. Yet the crudeness of the higher-class samurai's home was hidden behind a mud wall. Moreover, the size of the samurai homes varied according to the stipends of the owners, but the mud wall hid these inequalities and created a neighborhood with a uniform and unique appearance. This is part of the magic of a wall. If the walls had to be removed from the samurai neighborhood, the shabbiness of the houses would have been apparent.

The dominance of a fence or a hedge in the house design is a major peculiarity of the Japanese residence. In homes in Europe, and especially in America, such barriers are uncommon. A Japanese friend of mine who visited America to observe residential conditions said upon returning, "From now on we've got to stop putting walls and fences around Japanese houses." He was impressed by a row of American homes which had no partitions on the property lines or along the street so that the yards formed a continuous, refreshingly green lawn. My friend is convinced that our habit of splitting everything up, with each family tightly clutching its own postage-stamp-size garden, indicates a poverty of the Japanese spirit. But no matter how strongly my friend asserts his own individual opinion, it would be impossible to act upon his suggestion.

From the beginning there has been a fundamental structural difference between the western and the Japanese residence. A western home begins from the interior side of the front door of the building, whereas a Japanese home begins from the inside of the wall around the property. The garden is considered a component of the house. It is precisely because of this that from ancient times the relationship between the garden and the rooms of the house has been one of continuity, with each flowing into the other in an open fashion. In contrast, the front door of the western home is a visibly stout barrier which is one with the wall of the house; moreover it is often securely locked, perhaps with two or three different devices. The message is that one's yard is very much separate from one's house. Furthermore, the majority of western homes have no outlet to the yard other than the front and back doors. Most homeowners have no conception of the spirit behind a Japanese veranda. Clearly, the wall which serves to divide the interior and exterior of a western residence is directly analogous to the Japanese wall on the property line. In that sense, a fence or wall is an indispensable part of the average garden-equipped Japanese home.

Still, this outdoor partition, be it a fence, hedge or wall, serves different functions and gives rather different impressions according to the particular situation. The Japanese word for wall, "*kaki*," originally signified a solid enclosure of earth or stone and wood erected to surround a patch of ground. We know that this sort of *kaki* is quite old. A description of Japan in the third century in the Chinese *Wei chi*, or *Wei* Chronicle, records that the palace of the Yamatai empress Himiko was "fortified with a multistory rock wall." The character for "*kaki*" appears (with a slightly different pronunciation) some thousand years later during the war-torn medieval period in the term for a walled village (*kaito-shuraku*), which was protected by high earthworks, indicating that the word still at least partially signified a solid barrier.

Meanwhile, along with the transmission of Buddhism from China in the 6th century, more refined constructions such as plaster walls and woven bamboo fences, both large and small, entered Japan. These came to be known in Japan as *hei* and *kaki*, respectively. The type of

Iwamuro village in Nara Prefecture, one of the few remaining
walled villages (*kaito shuraku*) in Japan.

Shimenawa, a thick decorative rope found at most Shinto shrines and Buddhist temples.

wall known as a *hei* was made from earth or brick and was at first used exclusively for temples and the homes of the aristocracy. Even in later eras, it was not used to surround ordinary homes, with the limited exception of the homes of the samurai class. This may be related to the slightly distasteful nuance of coldness in the word which describes something, rather like a blindfold, that prevents one from even peeking in. Also, the common people were not endowed with the wealth which would require the protection of such a barrier.

Although the common people did not fear robbers or raiders, they did fear calamities which they thought were brought about by the return of spirits from the dead. No matter how high the wall, it could not keep out ghosts. Instead, the belief that the spirits of the dead could be miraculously appeased by placing a symbolic gift for them at the doorway had a very strong grip through the ages on the common people. A similar belief underlies the Shinto practice of hanging decorative straw and *shide* (pieces of paper folded in a stylized manner) from the *shimenawa* rope which surrounds the sacred precincts of a shrine, in

A small wooden fencelike partition (*kekkai*) sets off the inner area of the room (foreground), here used for accounting purposes, in this townhouse.

order to contain the spirits. The *shimenawa*, which is a thick rope suspended about a meter above the ground, can be thought of as the prototype of the "Japanese fence." Thus the *kaki*, like the *shimenawa*, does little to obstruct the view of the area inside it, and whoever wants to climb over it can very easily do so. It exists as a sort of demarcation of territory. Another example is the wooden fence found in Buddhist monasteries, called a *kekkai*, which separates the inner sanctum (the sacred) from the outer chambers (the secular). To this day, the basic characteristics of the *hei* and the *kaki* correspond to those of the effective barrier and the symbolic barrier.

Here it is necessary to say a few words about the fence (*saku*). The Japanese word originally signified a protective fence of vertical wooden stakes with horizontal stringers, but now includes not only wooden or metal picket fences but also chain-link and other sorts of barriers, as the English word "fence" does. Compared to the fragile *kaki*, a western fence functions more or less as a barrier. The western fence was originally developed as a means of closing in domestic animals such as cattle

A manicured hedge around a traditional farmhouse.

and sheep, and in old Japan the wooden fence surrounding a horse pad-
dock was known as a ''horse barrier'' (*komayose*). A Japanese fence is
not really designed to keep out human intruders.

Thus the Japanese wall (*kaki*) not only fails to keep out intruders, but
it is also rather ineffective as a visual barrier (the Japanese word for
''peeping'' is *kaima-miru*, literally, peeking through gaps in the *kaki*).
This is appropriate for the Japanese, who do not particularly care if
their activities fall under the gaze of the neighbors. Rather, they feel in-
secure if they are isolated from the neighbors. Among the Japanese the
group psychology assumes constant observation by others. Thus, for

crime prevention, the Japanese police recommend fences rather than walls.

The fact that the Japanese fence has now evolved into a hedge, a row of living shrubbery which serves to partition the household from the outer world, is interesting. The advantages of a hedge are that it makes the garden seem much larger because it does not seem to be a firm demarcation, and it provides greenery for the enjoyment of those in the street or as borrowed scenery for the neighboring garden. For passersby the seasonal changes are quite enjoyable. This sort of enclosure thus generates feelings of warmth and familiarity.

Gates

Recently gate doors have been selling very well in the department stores—including those with bronze or steel arabesque patterns with prices tags in the hundreds of thousands of yen. A few years back there was exploding demand for western-style beds and dining table sets, but now it seems there is a quiet boom in traditional Japanese gate doors. Considering the new level of affluence that Japan has attained, we might invoke the old saying "Well fed, well bred."

The Japanese single-family home almost always has a gate. Indeed, gates are not exclusively associated with single-family homes. In Kyoto, apartment buildings have sprung up with separate gates for each entrance. It might seem strange that a gate should be necessary for a fifth-floor apartment, but nevertheless it seems to have struck a chord with some apartment dwellers.

This sort of thing is not common in western residences. To begin with, there is usually no wall or fence surrounding the house, so no gate is needed. The country house of the English landed gentry, which seems to be the ideal house of the whole world, has a gate of some sort. But this is usually a simple affair which swings on a pair of posts sunk into the ground. Compared to the splendid mansion and vast lawn and garden to which the gate leads, it is quite a modest device. To Japanese eyes such a gate is hardly worthy of being called a gate, but looks rather more like a gap in the fence. In European cities, on the other hand, there are some magnificent public gateways, especially the central entrances to medieval walled cities. The arched gates of Rome and Paris, in particular, are outstanding works of art. In Europe, then, it can be said that cities have public gates, while private homes generally do not have gates. In contrast, Japanese cities, with only one or two exceptions, do not have public gates, but private residences do. Even today the homes of many ordinary people have gates.

A typical wooden slatted gate.

A modernized Japanese-style gate,
with a traditional auxiliary service
gate to the left.

A modern western-style gate.

In neighboring China, there have been city gates for many centuries. These gates are not only impressive, but they are also quite sturdy and can be closed quite securely. The primary function of the Chinese gate was to defend the city from the outside world. As we look at them today, we can feel once again their aura of stout security.

The historical genesis of the Japanese gate probably lies in the importation of the Chinese gate. Aside from the great capital city gates, such as the Suzakumon and Rashomon gates in Heijokyo (now Nara) and Heiankyo (now Kyoto), respectively, every temple and every nobleman's and courtier's residence had a gate. As for the common people's homes, judging from the many extant painted scrolls, neither farmhouses nor townhouses had gates. The gate definitely did not advance to the homes of common Japanese with the exception of some homes of the warrior class. This is probably because commoners had little need for one of the functions of the gate—the security of fastenable doors and fortifications. In other words, ordinary people did not have enough wealth to require them to defend it.

Yet the functions of the gate are not necessarily limited just to defense. The Chinese (and Japanese) character for gate (門) appears to consist of a pair of the character for doorway (戸). In the *Shuo-wen chi'eh-tzu*, the oldest Chinese dictionary of characters, we find that the derivation is that the doorway is half a gate. Going by both the shape of the characters and the *Shuo-wen chi'eh-tzu*, then, the difference between a doorway and a gateway might lie in whether it has one or two doors. But since doorways with two doors do in fact exist, this conclusion is too facile. All over the world, the size of a door matches fairly closely the dimensions of the human body, which allows us to say that a single door is normally sufficient for a person to enter or exit. Functionally speaking, then, if we ask what might necessitate dual doors, there are two possibilities: (1) more than one person goes in or out at the same time, or (2) something bigger than a person goes in or out. In the former case, one thinks about an organized group of people, such as a procession of nobles passing under a gate, or soldiers advancing in rows. In the latter case, one realizes that since the earliest times gateways have been constructed to allow horses and vehicles to pass. The people who rode in vehicles or on horses would have been those with special standing in the social order, and it is in this way that the gate came to be characteristically connected with social rank and status.

Thus we can regard a doorway as an entrance and exit for individual people, and a gateway as a passage for people with some sort of societal significance. In the Japanese language the word for "gate" (*mon*) is not limited to the gateway structure but appears in various compounds which refer to coherent social groups (such as the word for a household, *ichimon*, or for a believer or follower, *monto*). This would suggest that the word derives from such societal concepts. The presence of city gates in China or Europe can be an indication that urban organization or civic unity exist, just as the gate of a Chinese home might signify that a family resides there as a community. Although city gates were erected on the Chinese pattern in Japan, Japanese cities did not exhibit much urban unity or civic solidarity in ancient times. In the *Konjaku Monogatari* (Tales of Times Past), compiled in the 11th century, as well as in *Rashomon* (1917), a novel written by Ryunosuke Akutagawa (1892–1927), who was greatly attracted to the *Konjaku Monogatari*, the Rashomon Gate to the capital, Kyoto, had degenerated to the point where it had lost its value as a symbol of the authority or unity of the castle town, and had become a meaningless resting place for a pack of thieves and faceless passersby. In contrast, gates which were erected at the homes of the nobility and the royal guards, among whom clan solidarity was very strong, can be considered symbols of family solidarity. Thus it can be said that in Japanese society, clan unity based on kin relationships was stronger than the civic unity of the city, and the gate came to be an expression of the strength of that unity.

This sort of consciousness was not limited to kin groups. The merchants of medieval Kyoto united and built walls and gates which indicated the solidarity of the neighborhood, of people connected on the basis of territory. In the village of Sugaura at the northern tip of Lake Biwa in Shiga Prefecture, there is a village gate, something which is very unusual in Japan. It dates from medieval times, and used to bear a large inscription reading, ''Provincial constables prohibited from entry, we act on our own judgments.'' The villagers were firmly proclaiming themselves as a self-governing unit, determined to conduct their own judicial proceedings without relying on the *daimyo*, or feudal lords. These villagers had no simple ''solidarity,'' but a more complex type of community with power to punish transgressions. The gate was and still is the symbol of the community.

The union expressed by the gate could also extend further, beyond ties of blood and territory, to associations organized according to various schools of Buddhism or Shintoism. Buddhist priests in medieval times lived in what were called *shakka*, and these had gates. There is also the Japanese term ''*monzen-ichi o nasu*'' by which the stream of visitors seeking instruction from a learned priest is said to ''form a throng in front of the gate.'' Gates first appeared in front of the homes of ordinary

A typical *shimotaya* gate found at the homes of the self-employed in the Edo period.

people in the *shimotaya* design of the Edo period (1603–1867). The term "*shimotaya*" means "a household which has stopped trading," and its hallmarks were a small gate and a dense growth of trees and shrubs. These were the homes of the self-employed: instructors of such refined arts as flower arrangement and *koto* playing, physicians or schoolteachers. In those days the student would have to pass through the gate to meet the teacher, and to this day enrollment in an educational institution is referred to as "gate-entry" (*nyumon*). In the novel *Botchan* (1906) by Soseki Natsume (1867–1912), the loyal maidservant dreams that the university-educated Botchan will quickly become a distinguished man living in "a house with a gate." This suggests that many people still believed that houses with gates were reserved for the upper classes as late as the Meiji era (1868–1912).

From the modern perspective, priests, schoolteachers and physicians were purveyors of information, and they also functioned as the organizers of various associations. The diverse academies quickly organized into factions or cliques which brought both teachers and students into ever-stronger unions. Here again, the gate is clearly a symbol of group solidarity, especially since the Japanese word for "group" (*mon*) is the same word that is used for "gate."

Walking from house to house in a newly built residential subdivision, there is one feature of the gates which stands out. It may seem obvious, but virtually without exception every gate displays the name of the family on either a nameplate or a gatelight. Thus another role of the gate is to serve a sort of auxiliary structure on which to hang a nameplate. In narratives of the Edo period there are often accounts in which a

Yomeimon Gate at Toshogu Shrine in Tochigi Prefecture. This colorful gate commemorates the power of Tokugawa Ieyasu, the first Edo-period shogun.

challenger who has defeated the master of a martial arts academy removes the nameplate from the gate of the *dojo* (a training place for martial arts) and takes it home with him, after which the gate is presumably completely worthless. Another point is that the nameplate on the gate often includes only the surname, while a placard is commonly found over the front entrance, displaying the surname and given name of the head of the household. Thus the name on the gate is not that of an individual but rather a surname indicating the existence of a collective, a family household.

The modern home is not a "house" in the old-fashioned sense of having directly been passed on through many generations. Instead it has been reduced to a residence for a nuclear family comprising one couple and their children. The surname has thus come to indicate at most the few members of a family who live together in the dwelling; yet it is still a symbol of the family as a united entity, the "nuclear family community." In postwar Japanese society, as a result of the breakup of the extended family into nuclear families, intrafamilial bonds seem to have grown stronger. Indicative of this are some new phrases which have entered the national vocabulary, such as "mama's boy" and "education mother" (a mother who relentlessly drives her children toward academic success). Thus it seems that the demand among ordinary people for individual family homes is an expression of the aspiration to safeguard the nuclear family community, which in turn strengthens the bonds between parent and child. Today, then, the gate is a social proclamation that "the nuclear family named (Suzuki) lives here."

Locks

In the classic Japanese comic narrative called "The Thieves and the Optician's Shop," a pair of thieves stand in front of an optician's shop planning how they will break in. The shop boy, hearing what is going on, says to himself, "Aha, they're going to peek in through the keyhole," and straightway he puts a multifaceted eyepiece, which reflects multiple images, up against the opening. When the thief looks in, he sees a dozen errand boys practicing their penmanship. Recoiling in surprise, he motions to his accomplice to have a look. In the meantime, the errand boy quickly exchanges the lens for a magnifying glass, which makes him look like a giant.

"This place is haunted!" gasps the shaken accomplice. So the boss has another look. Meanwhile, the errand boy has put a lens for the nearsighted against the keyhole, backwards.

The boss thief says, "Hey, that's strange. Now it's too late to do the job!"

"What do you mean?"

"It's already the crack of dawn there in the distance."

Thieves often appear in traditional Japanese comic monologues. Maybe in the old days there really were a lot of them. But as this story shows, the merchants' homes were full of keyholes which could be peeped through. In a house like that, if a burglar wanted to enter, he could do so easily. As far as keeping them out, the old-fashioned Japanese house was not very reliable. Thus the errand boy was frantically trying to chase the thieves away with the only device he had on hand: lenses.

If a shelter is incomplete in such a manner, then naturally the theft rate increases, but it is also true that locks must not be neglected. For example, in 1969 the Kyoto prefectural police reported the most common form of entry taken by a burglar was through "unlocked doors," 31.2 percent, followed by "breaking glass," 18.6 percent; "breaking locks," 10.2 percent; and "locks picked," "no lock" and "miscellaneous," 8.8 percent. Aside from these, defective locks accounted for the remaining 30 percent or so of the cases, a rather startling figure. It seems that the Japanese could have prevented a great many robberies by paying a little more attention to their locks.

The history of the lock in Japan is surprisingly ancient. The records of the construction of Japan's oldest extant building, the Horyuji Temple in Nara, built in the 7th century, contain entries for both gate keys and storehouse keys. From what is known of the relationship between Japan and China at that time, it is probable that those locks and keys were imported from China. Yet subsequently, the lock and key made only negligible progress in Japan.

The diffusion of locks among the common people seems to have started three or four centuries ago in the late medieval and early Edo (1603–1867) eras, beginning with townspeople's storehouses. It is known there were many storehouse locks because there were several types of domestically produced products, including padlocks and "drum-shaped locks," and that they were decorated in various styles. It can be assumed that when people began to construct storehouses, the first Japanese locks were contrived. But these locks did not stop people from breaking into storehouses, which is to say that the early Japanese locks were not very effective. They may have looked quite adequate, but when it came to preventing thieves from entering, they proved to be of "typical Japanese construction"—not very solid. They were simply "symbolic seals," or symbols of wealth among the merchants, a far cry from a lock in the western, functional sense of the word.

Although locks were common in the tradesmen's neighborhoods where special structures served as repositories of wealth, locks and keys still bore virtually no relation to the homes and lives of the common people. Even today in agricultural villages there are many homes without locks. This may have been all right in a closed rural community, but what was done in the past to safeguard the average homes of the towns, where strangers were commonplace? The answer is simple. In those days there was someone inside the townhouse at all times who would remove the crossbar and open the door when someone else came home. Normally an apprentice, watchman or maidservant would spend the night in the house, and in many cases the elderly patriarch of the house would seldom leave the premises. If for some reason everyone had to be away, the family would request a friend, neighbor or relative to look

A traditional 19th-century lock.

after the house. This situation remained virtually unchanged until after World War II, constituting what can fairly be called a national residential crime prevention system. It was only storehouses, in which no one lived, that required locks.

Things changed significantly after the war. The major cause was the dissolution of the pre-war extended family pattern and the appearance of the nuclear family. The members of the nuclear family would often leave the home empty, and suitable caretakers could not be found on such a regular basis. Consequently, there was no choice but to rely on the lock and key. In the city of Kyoto, the zone where burglaries frequently occurred followed the "doughnut phenomenon" of movement of outward expansion to the suburban neighborhoods, which corresponded exactly to the growth and distribution of nuclear families.

Even so, Japanese locks continue to uphold the tradition established centuries ago, which is to say that many of them are rather cheap and crudely made. In recent years cylinder locks night latches, electronic locks and keys, and various new types of products have been marketed. But no matter how fine the lock, the traditional Japanese house remains accessible to burglars, since the structure itself can typically be penetrated at many points. If the lock is sturdy, the thieves remove the screws from the door jamb. If the door proves impassable, the burglars strip off the roof tiles or burrow under the floor space. Glass is obviously no barrier. There are cases of housebreakers removing floorboards and even breaking through walls. If someone really wants to get in, the nature of the Japanese house is to cooperate.

Since ancient times, the customary measure taken against burglary in Japan has been not to lock up with a key but to secure the door. In a traditional wooden house, a window has a hasp or a sliding bolt, the storm doors fit into a slot in the sill, the doors have bars or bolts, and each is carefully closed and secured. After everything has been checked, "locking the door" is the last step, as is fitting for a "symbolic seal." To prevent burglaries, the Japanese police recommend making the house "hard to unlock, hard to break into and hard to enter." The first means the lock and key, the second securing the doors and windows, and the last means keeping a dog, installing and maintaining a burglar alarm or alerting the neighbors. The police also say, "A bolt is better than a sturdy lock," for burglars are used to dealing with the locks which are on the market and are in any case mainly cheaply made, flimsy products. However, burglars may be hard put to figure out the working of a bolt which has been installed by the resident.

Many Japanese still live in such wooden structures, but more and more of them now enjoy the western-style security of ferroconcrete apartment buildings, where a single key effectively secures the residence. Ironically, the trouble with burglar-proof apartments is that interior noises cannot be heard from outside. If a burglar is confronted after he is inside, he may well turn upon his discoverer like a cornered animal and resort to violence in order to escape. For a long time Japan was able to stay behind the West in this respect, but the incidences of violent crimes inside shielded rooms has been rising lately, along with the spread of modern housing projects and apartment complexes. Thus if the vulnerability of the traditional Japanese house to intruders is the problem, simply converting to sturdier, ferroconcrete construction is not the whole answer.

The formula that was mentioned earlier—"hard to unlock, hard to break into, hard to enter"—needs an addition: "and easy to flee." When the occupant is inside and a burglar enters, the first reaction is to shout and run. The time-honored mantra is, of course, "Fire!" The desired effect is above all to escape. Confronting the intruder is very dangerous, for he is in a desperate position. The resident is likely to know just enough to get himself into trouble, and not enough to get himself out.

In terms of shelter, the typical wooden house of Japan is admittedly full of cracks, but by the same token it is easy to flee in times of need. There is always the back door, and then there is the veranda, which gives the traditional house an advantage or two over most apartment dwellings since most Japanese apartments do not have back doors. Jumping out the window is not advisable above the ground floor. Many look to the balcony, but it is usually separated from the neighboring balcony by a stout partition. There has been a trend toward building thinner partitions as a provision for just such an emergency, but people, especially the Japanese, often fill their balconies with all sorts of things that make them unreliable crisis routes.

From the point of view of the ease or difficulty of getting in and out, residential shelters can be categorized into these four types: (1) traditional wooden homes (easy entry, easy exit); (2) ferroconcrete apartments (difficult entry, difficult exit); (3) rat trap (easy entry, difficult exit) and (4) reverse rat trap (difficult entry, easy exit).

Evaluated in terms of the crime prevention measures, the most desirable pattern for a residence is the last one, the "reverse rat trap." The basic features of this pattern are (1) a strong lock, (2) secure doors and windows throughout the house and (3) neighbors close by. Simply installing a burglar alarm on an electric pole can keep intruders at a distance. These cover "difficult entry." The fourth step is to plan an "easy exit" from the structure. The necessary design elements are (1) a back door or service entrance in addition to the main entryway, (2) a largish window in the bathroom or elsewhere and (3) in an apartment, balconies, both front and rear, which interconnect with the neighbors' premises.

These precautions do much more than just defend one's self and one's property against criminals. Common sense would dictate that the same precautions ensure an easy escape in case of earthquake or fire. As Japanese cities become more and more overcrowded, constant attention must be paid to safety measures for each individual residence. At this point, as we look forward to the 21st century, that may well be the single most important consideration for the Japanese residence.

Acknowledgments

The cooperation of Shigeyoshi Suzuki, the editor and driving force behind this book, and Kodansha International, the publisher, have made this English edition possible. Alan Brender applied his apt hand to the task of polishing the English translation with skill and discretion. Barry Lancet was instrumental in assembling all the pieces and bringing the book to its present form.

I also wish to extend my gratitude to my Japanese publisher, Iwanami Shoten, who supported my decision to seek an English-language publisher; to Yoshitaka Itohara, who consented on very short notice to allow his home to be used for the front jacket of this volume; to Shigeo Okamoto, whose excellent photographic skills captured the understated beauty of Mr. Itohara's residence; to Hikone-shi, in Shiga Prefecture, for permission to use the photograph of Genkyu-en which appears on the back jacket; and to Neil Warren, a practicing architect in Tokyo, who checked the technical aspects of this translation.

I am indebted to the following people and institutions for graciously allowing photographs in their possession to be reproduced in this volume. Names are listed here alphabetically. The page numbers on which the photographs appear are in parentheses immediately after each listing.

Aizu Bange-cho Kyoiku Iinkai (94), Byodoin (158–59 Both), Daitoku-ji Temple (167), Gifu Castle (119), Higashi Osaka Kyoiku Iinkai (105 Both), Shinji Horiuchi (44), Horyuji Temple (14), Hyakumangoku Bunka-en (109), The Imperial Household Agency (74 Top, 136–37, 165), Ise Shrine (13), Yoshitaka Itohara/Photo by Shigeo Okamoto (86–87), Keiichiro Iwase (103 Bottom), Izumo Shrine (12, 23, 182), Jisho-ji (54), Katsura Detached Palace (70), Chuji Kawashima (24 top, 35 Both, 89), Kinkakuji (118), Kodai-ji Temple (174, 175), Kyoto Imperial Palace (45, 65, 66), Manshu-in (61 Both), Ministry of Education (63), Akira Mita (18), Shigekata Mori (154), Masatoshi Nasu (46), Nihon Minka-en (47, 53, 183), Nikko Toshogu (191), Nishi Hongan-ji (30–31, 68–69, 81), Heitaro Ogawa (29, 111), Omote Senke School of Tea (100), Sankeien (122, 173 Bottom), Riemon Sato (110), Shikoku Minka Museum (80), Sumiya (52 Bottom, 72), Kanzo Takahashi (149), Jirozaemon Takanashi (104), Miyuki Takano (16, 147), Atsuko Tanaka (51, 90, 132), Hiroshi Tokikuni (38–39), Toro Museum (74 Bottom, 75, 113), Towadako Kyoiku Iinkai (25), Kyubei Yoshijima (17), Takashi Yoshimura (96), and Usa Shrine (156).

JAPANESE HISTORICAL PERIODS

Jomon	10,000 B.C.–300 B.C.
Yayoi	300 B.C.–A.D. 300
Kofun/Tumulus	4 c–7 c
Asuka	593–710
Nara	710–94
Heian	794–1185
Kamakura	1185–1333
Muromachi	1333–1573
Edo	1603–1867
Meiji	1868–1912
Taisho	1912–25
Showa	1925–89